Dr. Robert Jeffress, *The 10*

"In this wise and inspirational book, Dr. Robert Jeffress explores ten biblical rules for life. In a world that's lost its way, we can still live in a way that honors God and experience a blessed life. If you're interested in the unseen but very real spiritual laws that shape our daily lives, *The 10* is a must-read."

Dr. Tommy Barnett, global pastor of Dream City Church of Phoenix, copastor of Los Angeles Dream Center, and chancellor of Southeastern University

"*The 10* spans the centuries from Sinai to our present day, giving a fresh and relevant application of God's timeless commandments. Read it and share it with your friends!"

Dr. Erwin W. Lutzer, pastor emeritus of The Moody Church, Chicago

"I knew *The 10* would be a good book, but I was not prepared for how readable and gripping it is. You will have a hard time putting this book down! If you have struggled with legalism, this book will set you free. If you are looking for a book on the Law to give to your friends, this is it. Thank you, Dr. Jeffress."

Dr. R. T. Kendall, former minister of Westminster Chapel

Praise for *Courageous*

"With all the uncertainty in our world right now, this new book by my friend Robert Jeffress is a welcome encouragement for believers. His Bible-based tips on thriving during challenging times are not only practical and easy to understand but will help you to stand strong in your faith and live victoriously."

Robert Morris, founding lead senior pastor of Gateway Church and bestselling author of *The Blessed Life, Frequency,* and *Beyond Blessed*

"When it comes to living out biblical principles, we quickly discover we're in an unfriendly culture. Ephesians 5:11 tells us to 'Have nothing to do with the fruitless deeds of darkness,' so how then do we build bridges to skeptics and cynics? How do we win wicked people with antagonistic agendas to the side of our Savior? In *Courageous*, Dr. Jeffress shows us page-by-page how to live as winsome and effective ambassadors for Jesus Christ, all so that the perishing will come to salvation and God will receive the glory! I give this book a double thumbs-up!"

Joni Eareckson Tada, Joni and Friends International Disability Center

"No book title ever fit its author's personality better than this one. One of the words I often use to describe Robert Jeffress is *courageous*. As a former pastor of First Baptist in Dallas, I have been privileged to watch time and again his courageous yet loving leadership in daily action. This book is not some self-help treatise. These principles have been beaten out on the anvil of the author's own personal and practical experience. Read it . . . and reap!"

O. S. Hawkins, former pastor of First Baptist Church, Dallas, and author of the bestselling Code series of Christian devotionals

"My friend Robert Jeffress has demonstrated courage time and again by boldly preaching God's Word in the pulpit and answering tough critics in the media. In these pages, he outlines practical survival strategies that will help us courageously navigate the storms of life. Through powerful biblical examples and present-day testimonies, Robert reminds us that the wisdom and supernatural ability God has provided us as believers is more than enough to defeat the enemy's strategy."

James Robison, founder and president of LIFE Outreach International, Fort Worth, Texas

Praise for *Invincible*

"Are you having difficulty believing you are a conqueror in Jesus Christ? In *Invincible* you will be encouraged to face the big mountains in your life and learn to live a life of boldness for God. You will benefit significantly from Dr. Jeffress's biblical insights on how to overcome the doubt, guilt, anxiety, discouragement, fear, bitterness, materialism, loneliness, lust, and grief that are ravishing your life."

Jason Jimenez, founder of Stand Strong Ministries and bestselling author of *Challenging Conversations*

"There is often pressure in church to act as if you have it all together. 'Don't bring your doubt, anxiety, fear, or guilt in this place!' *Invincible* pushes back against this kind of phony faith and gives us the freedom to acknowledge our struggles. With humor, compassion, and practical advice, Dr. Jeffress provides a way to overcome the mountains we all face and encourage one another on our faith journey. This book is for real people who want real change."

Michael C. Sherrard, pastor and author of *Why You Matter*

THE
10

THE
10

How to Live and Love in a World That Has Lost Its Way

Dr. Robert Jeffress

BakerBooks

a division of Baker Publishing Group
Grand Rapids, Michigan

Published by Baker Books
a division of Baker Publishing Group
Grand Rapids, Michigan
www.bakerbooks.com

Printed in the United States of America

Library of Congress Cataloging-in-Publication Control Number: 2023002261
ISBN 978-1-5409-0049-4 (cloth)
ISBN 978-1-4934-4326-0 (ebook)

Unless otherwise indicated, Scripture quotations are from the (NASB®) New American Standard Bible, copyright © 1960, 1971, 1977, 1995 by The Lockman Foundation. Used by permission. All rights reserved. www.lockman.org.

Scripture quotations labeled KJV are from the King James Version of the Bible.

Scripture quotations labeled MSG are from THE MESSAGE, copyright © 1993, 2002, 2018 by Eugene H. Peterson. Used by permission of NavPress. All rights reserved. Represented by Tyndale House Publishers, Inc.

Scripture quotations labeled NIV are from THE HOLY BIBLE, NEW INTERNATIONAL VERSION®, NIV® Copyright © 1973, 1978, 1984, 2011 by Biblica, Inc.® Used by permission. All rights reserved worldwide.

Scripture quotations labeled NLT are from the Holy Bible, New Living Translation, copyright © 1996, 2004, 2007, 2013, 2015 by Tyndale House Foundation. Used by permission of Tyndale House Publishers, Inc., Carol Stream, Illinois 60188. All rights reserved.

Scripture quotations labeled TLB are from The Living Bible, copyright © 1971. Used by permission of Tyndale House Publishers, Inc., Carol Stream, Illinois 60188. All rights reserved.

All italics in direct Scripture quotations are the author's emphasis.

Published in association with Yates & Yates, www.yates2.com.

Baker Publishing Group publications use paper produced from sustainable forestry practices and post-consumer waste whenever possible.

23 24 25 26 27 28 29   7 6 5 4 3 2 1

Contents

Age-Old Commands

Not long ago, I purchased a new car. I wasn't thrilled about going to the dealership, haggling over the price, and waiting for what seemed like all day to complete the paperwork. But I enjoyed taking in the new car smell as I test-drove a few models and figured out some of the bells and whistles—hands-free driving, self-parking, a cappuccino machine. . . . Okay, maybe not a cappuccino machine, but it seems like there's nothing today's cars can't do!

After I settled on a car and handed over my life savings to the dealership, do you know what the sales associate had the nerve to do? He gave me a book filled with instructions from the manufacturer about how I was supposed to operate the car I now owned. For example, in chapter 1, verse . . . I mean, page 7, the manufacturer said, "Don't text and drive." Who did they think they were, trying to stifle my right to free speech? Or how about this, on page 15: "Never remove the coolant reservoir cap while the engine is running." They provided no explanation, expecting me to take it on faith that removing that cap is a bad idea. Or how about this one: "Always drive and ride with your seat back upright." So why did they design my car with reclining seats? I didn't know who these people thought they were, but they didn't have a right to tell me how to run my car.

It's a silly illustration, I know, but it makes an important point. Obviously, the car manufacturer didn't prepare this book of instructions to limit my fun; they prepared it for my well-being and enjoyment. The manufacturer designed every inch of my car. They knew under what conditions it would operate most efficiently. They provided an owner's manual to let me know how to get the best performance out of my vehicle, make it last, and keep me safe. Sure, it's my car, and I can run it however I want to. But if I disregard the manufacturer's instructions, I do so at my own peril.

In a similar way, God designed and created each of us. He knows what makes us run best and what causes us to sputter, spit, and stop. And God gave us His Word, the Bible—an operating manual that tells us how to get the most out of life.

Many people believe God is the great killjoy in the sky and the Bible is His rulebook He throws at us whenever we step out of line. That's not true at all. In fact, the opposite is true: God wants us to enjoy life, and He gave us the Bible for our well-being. We can ignore God's Word, but we do so at our own risk because it shows us the secret to a blessed life. But to enjoy that blessedness, we must follow its instructions. And the best place to start is with God's most foundational instructions: the Ten Commandments.

The Ten Commandments—God's Invitation to a Blessed Life

Before we take a look at God's operating rules for a blessed life, let's take a little quiz. Quickly—without checking Google or your Bible—name as many of the Ten Commandments as you can. Go ahead . . . I'll wait.

How did you do? If you struggled to remember them, you're not alone. According to a *USA Today* poll, 60 percent of Americans can't name five of the Ten Commandments.[1] In fact, only 14 percent can name all ten.[2] I think it's safe to say that our society—including many Christians—has lost sight of these fundamental rules for living.

Only a generation ago, it was generally accepted that the Ten Commandments were the foundation of our nation's legal system.[3] Many of us grew up with these rules posted in our schools, not to mention the depictions of the Ten Commandments in the Supreme Court and other government buildings. So why don't we know them anymore?

In recent years, the prevailing view has changed so that anything related to the Bible and morality is seen as obsolete. We're obsessed with our freedom to believe and do anything we want. Many people consider the Ten Commandments to be an oppressive code of behavior from a bygone era—an archaic collection of "thou shalt nots" that no longer apply in today's world.

Yet, far from what most people think, the Ten Commandments weren't given to restrict our freedom but to enhance our happiness. They serve as guardrails that keep our lives on track. These timeless truths invite us into the blessing of a love relationship with God and the resulting spillover into our relationships with others.

I'm convinced that our lack of application of the Ten Commandments is responsible for the deterioration of our nation, our churches, our homes, and our personal lives. In a culture like ours, where moral confusion reigns, where "what is right is wrong and what is wrong is right" (Isa. 5:20 TLB), we desperately need to get back to the basics of morality—to simple, clear answers about what it means to live and love in a world that has lost its way. And that's just what the Ten Commandments provide.

Historical Setting of the Ten Commandments

Before we dive into our study, let's look briefly at the setting of the Ten Commandments. These commands came out of one of the greatest events in the Old Testament: the exodus of God's people from Egypt.

The book of Exodus tells us how God miraculously delivered His people from slavery and then rescued them from the pursuing Egyptian army. They crossed the Red Sea and headed to the promised land. The Lord led His people through the wilderness for three months, until they came to the base of Mount Sinai.[4]

God called Moses to the top of the mountain to receive the law that would govern the new nation (Exod. 19:1–6). The people understood there needed to be a mediator between God and them. At that point in time, the go-between was Moses. He was a type, or foreshadowing, of Jesus Christ. The Bible says, "There is one God, and one mediator also between God and men, the man Christ Jesus" (1 Tim. 2:5). But at that time, Moses served as the mediator between God and His people.

You may remember this scene as it was dramatically portrayed by Charlton Heston in the classic film *The Ten Commandments*.[5] In the midst of a dense cloud, accompanied by thunder and lightning, smoke and fire, a trumpet blast and an earthquake, God delivered the Ten Commandments (Exod. 19:9–20:22).

The "Ten Commandments" is the phrase we use to describe the list in Exodus 20:1–17 and Deuteronomy 5:6–21, but that's not how the ancient Hebrews referred to these commands. In Exodus 34:28 and Deuteronomy 4:13 and 10:4, the Hebrew phrase is *aseret ha'devarim*, which literally means "Ten Words." Translated into Greek, it is *deka* (ten) *logos* (word)—the Decalogue, which it is often called.

In Deuteronomy 5, Moses repeated the Ten Commandments and reminded the people, "These words the LORD spoke to all your assembly at the mountain from the midst of the fire, of the cloud and of the thick gloom, with a great voice, and He added no more. He wrote them on two tablets of stone and gave them to me" (v. 22). It's important to note that God communicated His most basic rules for living both audibly and in written form.

The Lord specified the blessing of the Decalogue in Deuteronomy 5:29: "Oh that they had such a heart in them, that they would fear Me and keep all My commandments always, *that it may be well with them and with their sons forever!*"

Moses confirmed the blessing of obeying these Ten Words: "You shall walk in all the way which the LORD your God has commanded you, *that you may live and that it may be well with you, and that you may prolong your days in the land which you will possess*" (v. 33).

For the Israelites, this blessing meant a homeland marked by peace, justice, and morality. Those same blessings are available to us if we obey God's commandments. This doesn't mean our lives will be free from disease, disappointment, and death. Those blessings will come in the new heaven and new earth (Rev. 21:4). But it does mean if more people obeyed the Ten Commandments, we'd see a remarkable change in our personal lives and in our communities.

Why Did God Give the Ten Commandments?

You may be saying, "Wait a minute, Pastor. All this talk about the Ten Commandments is nice, but do we still have to obey these rules? After all, the Bible says Christians are under grace, not the law."

That's a good question. If you've been a Christian for a while, you're probably familiar with the apostle Paul's words in Romans 6:15: "We are not under law but under grace." The apostle John pointed out this distinction between the law and grace: "The Law was given through Moses; grace and truth were realized through Jesus Christ" (John 1:17). Since the Ten Commandments are part of the Old Testament law, it's completely understandable if you're wondering, *Why should we obey the Ten Commandments today?*

To answer that question, we need to understand the purpose of the law.

The Purpose of the Law

Many Christians view the Old Testament law negatively. But the apostle Paul also wrote, "the Law is holy" (Rom. 7:12) and "the Law is good, if one uses it lawfully" (1 Tim. 1:8). There's nothing wrong with the Old Testament law. It's just that the law, strictly speaking, is limited.

So what is the purpose of the Old Testament law?

- The law reveals God's righteous character, but it can't make us righteous (Gal. 2:21).
- The law is a tutor to teach us about the Savior, but it can't save us (3:24).
- The law detects spiritual death, but it can't make us alive (v. 21).

We can think of it this way: Imagine the Old Testament law is like a mirror, which, according to the apostle James, is exactly what it's like (1:23–25). What's the purpose of a mirror? When we look in a mirror, we can see the dirt on our faces. (And these days, my mirror also reveals a lot more wrinkles and gray hair!) The mirror shows us what needs to be cleaned, but it can't remove any of the dirt.

The Old Testament law is like a mirror that shows us how dirty our lives really are. When we look into the law, we see the perfection God demands and realize all the ways we fall short of God's righteousness (Rom. 3:23). Like a mirror, the Old Testament law reveals that we are dirty, but it is absolutely powerless to clean us up.

Does that mean the law is bad? Not at all. The law is doing exactly what God designed it to do. The law reflects God's holiness and reveals how much we need His forgiveness and salvation. The purpose of the law is to lead us to the only thing that can remove our sin and guilt—the forgiveness of God through Jesus Christ that cleanses us (Isa. 1:18).

Did God believe the Israelites could actually keep the law? Of course not. God knew we could never keep the standards of the law. Nowhere in the Bible is the idea that we can earn our salvation by keeping the law. That's impossible. That's why God instituted a sacrificial system with the understanding that His people would need forgiveness.

Some Christians think the Old Testament teaches we're saved by the law and the New Testament teaches we're saved by grace. That isn't true. We find grace in the very first pages of the Old Testament. In Genesis 3, after Adam and Eve sinned and sewed together those ill-fitting coverings of fig leaves, they experienced God's grace when He killed an animal, took the skin, and covered the first couple. We see grace and faith in Genesis 15:6, which says Abraham "believed in the LORD; and He reckoned it to him as righteousness."

Every believer is saved the same way, whether it was in the Old or the New Testament. Salvation is by grace, which is appropriated through faith in Jesus Christ (Eph. 2:8). God gave the law not to save His people but to teach them how to live. The law, including the Ten Commandments, was given for the personal well-being of God's people.

The Letter of the Law

Generally speaking, Christians aren't obligated to obey the Old Testament law, but there are some laws that still apply to Christians today—not to earn our eternity in heaven but to increase our enjoyment of life here on earth. To determine whether we are to heed a specific Old Testament law, we can see if that law is repeated in the New Testament and applied to followers of Christ.

For example, the ceremonial law that prohibits wearing garments made from mixed materials (Lev. 19:19; Deut. 22:11) isn't found in the New Testament. Or consider the laws surrounding the Jewish sacrificial system. Are we obligated to follow those? No. The New Testament is clear that Jesus, the perfect Lamb of God, sacrificed Himself once for all on the cross (Heb. 10:1–18).

In fact, most of the laws in the Old Testament books of Exodus, Leviticus, Numbers, and Deuteronomy aren't applicable to Christians today because we're no longer "under law but under grace," as Paul said in Romans 6:15. In these cases, we are freed from the letter of the law.

However, as believers in Christ, we aren't freed from the law of love. Let's take a deeper look at what that means.

The Law of Love

We see the law of love as a recurring theme throughout the Bible. God issued this command in Deuteronomy 6:5: "You shall love the LORD your God with all your heart and with all your soul and with all your might." And in Leviticus 19:18, the Lord said, "You shall love your neighbor as yourself."

When we turn to the New Testament, we find Jesus uttering those same words (Matt. 22:37–39). He concluded, "On these two commandments depend the whole Law and the Prophets" (v. 40), referring to the totality of God's Word.[6] This idea of loving God and others was picked up by Paul and other New Testament writers, placing all Christians under the obligation to obey those two Old Testament commands: love God and love your neighbor.

The same is true for the Ten Commandments. The first few commandments about acknowledging the one and only God and giving Him honor in worship exclusively are peppered throughout the New Testament. You can hardly take a bite out of the Gospels, the letters of Paul, or the writings of the other apostles without tasting the first few statements of the Ten Commandments. In His Sermon on the Mount (Matt. 5–7), Jesus selected three commandments—against murder, adultery, and bearing false witness—as representatives of the Ten Commandments. He applied them for His disciples, from the first century to the twenty-first century and beyond. In fact, the only commandment not repeated in the New Testament is the fourth commandment about keeping the Sabbath, which we'll address later.

While believers today aren't bound to obey every Old Testament law, we are to obey the Ten Commandments because the Lord preserved and repeated them in the New Testament.

The Ten Words

It's well past time for us not only to tack the Ten Commandments back on our schoolroom walls but, more importantly, to tack them on our hearts and minds. That's what this book is about. In the chapters that follow, we're going to talk about what the commandments mean, how they apply to our lives, and why they're God's method for freeing us to experience blessings we could never imagine. So let's look quickly at these commandments.

The First Commandment: Esteem God Alone

Almost from the beginning, we've been told we don't need God—instead, we can (and should) be like God. That was the big lie Satan told the first couple in the garden of Eden (Gen. 3:5), and we've been living with the consequences ever since. So the first commandment sets straight the truth about who is and who isn't God. All the other commandments flow out of this truth. We are to have no other gods before the Lord God (Exod. 20:3).

The Second Commandment: Worship God Only

If God is the only true God, then He alone deserves our worship. This is the point of the second commandment (Exod. 20:4–6). Today, we might not carve idols shaped like golden calves, but we can have idols in our lives. If we're not careful, we can easily let our affection for people or possessions take the central place in our hearts reserved for God alone. If we do, we place ourselves under God's judgment. But if we obey this command to worship God only, we place ourselves under His blessing.

The Third Commandment: Revere God's Name

When we hear the name of God or Jesus used in a derogatory way, usually with an exclamation point, we think, *Shame on you for taking the Lord's name in vain* (Exod. 20:7). But even if you've never uttered that curse or used Jesus's name in that way, you're just as likely to be guilty of violating the third commandment because dishonoring God's name involves a lot more than only cursing.

The Fourth Commandment: Value God's Day

In the fourth commandment, God calls us to set aside a day to give Him our undivided attention. He commands us to reserve one day each week when we cease our work and create a time of rest and worship (Exod. 20:8–11). But since this is the only commandment not reiterated in the New Testament, what does valuing God's day mean for Christians today?

The Fifth Commandment: Honor Your Parents

No matter the circumstances of our upbringing, every Christian is required to obey the fifth commandment to honor our parents (Exod. 20:12). What makes this command unique is that it's the only one with a specific promise from God. How might that promise be fulfilled for us today? And how do we honor our parents? It's more than just obeying them when living in their home.

The Sixth Commandment: Preserve Life

The sixth commandment is often rendered, "Thou shalt not kill" (Exod. 20:13 KJV), giving the impression that taking any life violates God's standard. If that's the case, how do we square that with God's commands for the taking of life in capital punishment or warfare? There has to be more going on here—and there is. The sixth commandment is against murder. But where do things like suicide and hatred fall under this command?

The Seventh Commandment: Keep Marriage Holy

Many modern definitions of *family* are at odds with the biblical view of a lifelong marriage between one man and one woman. But even with those who hold a different perspective, there's near-universal agreement that adultery is the single greatest threat to family stability, which is why God issued the seventh commandment about keeping marriage holy (Exod. 20:14).

The Eighth Commandment: Respect the Property of Others

In recent years, American streets have been filled with people violating God's eighth commandment against stealing or destroying another person's property (Exod. 20:15). It might be hard for any one of us to make much of a difference in preventing theft on a large scale, such as looting or corporate fraud, but all of us can do something about it on a small scale, beginning with teaching our children to respect the property of others.

The Ninth Commandment: Protect the Reputation of Others

James said our speech is like a cozy campfire that, if left unattended, can cause a devastating forest fire (3:5). In his day, torching someone's reputation was a slow burn, since gossip generally traveled one person at a time. But with today's social media, a spark of gossip can travel around the world instantly, engulfing someone's reputation. The Lord made it clear in the ninth commandment that Christians are not to "bear false witness against [our] neighbor"; rather, we should do all we can to protect their reputation (Exod. 20:16).

The Tenth Commandment: Control Yourself and Be Content

The tenth commandment (Exod. 20:17) has to do with controlling our desires and being content with what the Lord has provided. We live in a world that insists we should have more, more, more. This is played out in what the Lord called "coveting," the envy that wells up in us when we see our friends and neighbors succeed while it seems like we're stuck. This chapter will look at ways we can combat covetousness and learn how to control ourselves and be content.

The Freedom of God's Commandments

There are plenty of reasons we should obey the Ten Commandments today.

First, *God is our Lord*. It couldn't be any clearer than what is written in Exodus 20:1–2: "Then God spoke all these words, saying, 'I am the LORD your God.'" The Ten Commandments aren't impersonal laws from a distant deity; they're rules on how to have a blessed life from the heart of a Father to His sons and daughters. The Ten Commandments are characterized by love and grace—the characteristics at the center of God's heart.

Second, *God has set us free*. The Lord said, "I am the LORD your God, who brought you out of the land of Egypt, out of the house of slavery" (v. 2). God's great desire for His people, then and now, is for us to live in freedom (John 8:32). But freedom requires boundaries. Like a life-giving river, freedom is designed to stay within its banks. If a river exceeds its banks, it becomes a destructive and deadly flood. Without boundaries, freedom turns into chaos. The Ten Commandments are our boundaries, but we must choose to stay inside them.

Finally, *God loves us and we love Him.* The apostle John said we love God because He first loved us (1 John 4:19). And if we love God, then we'll obey God. Jesus made this point clear in John 14:15: "If you love Me, you will keep My commandments." John picked up Jesus's words and told his readers, "For this is the love of God, that we keep His commandments; and His commandments are not burdensome" (1 John 5:3).

God's commandments are freeing. And that's a promise you can stake your life on.

1

The First Commandment: Esteem God Alone

You shall have no other gods before Me.

Exodus 20:3

In my many years of pastoring, I've married my share of couples. Every wedding I've officiated has been a blessed celebration, especially when the bride and groom are believers in Christ Jesus.

I first met my wife, Amy, when we were both twelve years old. Through our years of dating in high school and college we had our ups and downs, breakups and reconciliations. But on July 30, 1977, I made a unique and unbreakable promise. When Amy and I exchanged our vows during our wedding, I promised to love and cherish her, to place her above my own needs and wants, and to forsake all other women. In fact, I promised "to have and to hold" her "for better, for worse, for richer, for poorer, in sickness and in health." In short, I made a vow to *esteem* her all the days of my life. And while I can't claim to have done so perfectly throughout the decades of our marriage, on the whole I have kept my vow. She still keeps me around.

You might be thinking, *That's great, Pastor. Congratulations. But what does this have to do with the first commandment?* Well, in a word: everything. Whatever else the first commandment might mean, at its core is the love relationship between God and His people and their requirement to esteem God alone.

What It Means to Esteem Someone

Before we can obey the first commandment—to have no other gods before God—we need to understand what it means to esteem someone. *Merriam-Webster* defines *esteem* as "the regard in which one is held, *especially*: high regard." It is "to set a high value on: regard and prize accordingly."[1] In other words, to esteem someone is to assign great worth or value to that person.

The Old Testament uses two Hebrew words for "esteem." The first is *arak*, meaning "to arrange things and put them in order." When applied to a person, the idea is to give priority to someone by placing them first in a series. The other is *chashab* and means "to regard, repute, or value." Both *arak* and *chashab* are easy to understand if you've participated in a band or choir. There are any number of students playing the same instrument or singing the same part. My high school band didn't have a place for an accordion player, my preferred instrument, but let's say I played trumpet. There's a row of trumpet players in the band, but there can only be one first chair player. Because the band director regards the talent of the first chair player as better than all the other trumpet players, the first chair player receives the esteemed position for the trumpet. The same is true in sports. For example, there's a starting quarterback and a second-string quarterback.

The Greek word translated as "esteem" (*hegeomai*) follows along the same idea. It means to place someone in a leading position, and therefore that person should be accorded the utmost respect.

We see this idea of esteeming someone played out in Scripture between the husband and children of the Proverbs 31 woman. The writer of this proverb, King Lemuel, started off with the highest praise for her. Not only was she "an excellent wife" whose "worth is far above jewels" (v. 10), but Lemuel also said, "The heart of her husband trusts in her" (v. 11). President Ronald Reagan used to quote the proverb, "Trust, but verify."[2] However, when you think about it, that's an oxymoron. If you trust someone, you don't have to verify their integrity. That was certainly true of the husband of this excellent wife. Instead of looking over his wife's shoulder, checking in to see if she was being productive, notice where her husband spent his days. He was "known in the gates" and "[sat] among the elders of the land," where he transacted legal and judicial affairs (v. 23). He esteemed his wife by placing his trust in her, and she esteemed him by enhancing his standing among the people.

But King Lemuel wasn't through esteeming this excellent woman. He wrote, "Her children rise up and bless her; her husband also [blesses her], and he praises her, saying: 'Many daughters have done nobly, but you excel them all'" (vv. 28–29). Lemuel concluded, "Charm is deceitful and beauty is vain, but a woman who fears the LORD, she shall be praised. Give her the product of her hands, and let her works praise her in the gates" (vv. 30–31).

That's what it means to esteem someone—to praise them, bless them, trust them, value them, respect them to the utmost, and prize them above all.

Why We Should Esteem God Alone

Why should we esteem God? The answer to the question seems obvious. You might be thinking, *Well, duh! Of course we should esteem God. He's God, after all.* You'd be right. But there's more to be said about why we should esteem God alone, just as there's more to be said about God being God.

Let's take a closer look at Exodus 20:1–3: "Then God spoke all these words, saying, 'I am the LORD your God, who brought you out of the land of Egypt, out of the house of slavery. You shall have no other gods before Me.'"

In Exodus 20:2, the Lord said the Israelites should obey the Ten Commandments because of *who He is* ("I am the LORD your God") and *what He has done* ("who brought you out of the land of Egypt, out of the house of slavery"). God knew the Israelites were about to enter into a land in which many gods were worshiped. And He was saying, "Regardless of what other people are doing around you, you are not to serve any other god than Me."

Honestly, when we read that it can strike us the wrong way. We wonder, "God, what's wrong with You? Why are You so petty and paranoid? Why are You so fearful that people are going to worship another god? Are You that self-centered that You would direct all worship to Yourself?"

Remember, God's laws were given not for His benefit but for our benefit. There's a reason God says to esteem only Him. In verse 2, the Lord told us two fundamental qualities about who He is and two fundamental activities He's done for us. If we knew nothing else about God, these four reasons are sufficient for us to esteem Him alone.

God Is Creator

The idea of God as *Creator* is found in the word "LORD" (Exod. 20:2). When this word appears in small caps in the Old Testament, it's the English translation of the Hebrew word *Yahweh*, which can be rendered "I AM WHO I AM" (3:14). The idea is that God is self-existent, eternal, and sovereign. He is the uncreated Creator of everything seen and unseen—from the billions of stars in the sky to the billions of starfish in the sea. John said, "All things came into being through Him, and apart from Him nothing came into being that has come into being" (John 1:3).

Astronomers have peered into the cosmos and seen four billion light-years away. That's twenty-five septillion miles—the number 25 with twenty-four zeros trailing behind. To give you an idea of how large the universe is, if you could travel at the speed of light, 186,000 miles a second, it would take you 1.3 seconds to travel from the earth to the moon, 8.3 seconds to travel from the earth to the sun, and almost 200,000 *years* to travel across the Milky Way galaxy.[3] And our galaxy is just one of billions of galaxies.

Where did our galaxy or any of the other galaxies come from? The late physicist Stephen Hawking thought he knew the answer to that question. He developed a theory called the Theory of Everything (TOE). He said, "My proposal is the statement that the universe is a closed system. We don't need to suppose that there's something outside the universe which is not subject to its law. It is the claim that the laws of science are sufficient to explain the universe." In other words, all that exists can be explained through mathematical equations. If that's so, then where does God fit in? On that question, Hawking admitted ignorance. "Even if we had a TOE, we would still be left with one final question. What is it that breathes fire into the equations and makes a universe for them to describe? If I knew that then I would know everything important."[4]

We know the answer to Hawking's question. And the answer isn't an It but a Who—the Creator God, revealed to us in the pages of Scripture and in the person of Jesus Christ. In Colossians 1:15–17, Paul made it clear that Christ created and sustains the entire universe: "He is the image of the invisible God, the firstborn of all creation. For by Him all things were created, both in the heavens and on earth, visible and invisible, whether thrones or dominions or rulers or authorities—all things have been created through Him and for Him. He is before all things, and in Him all things hold together."

God Is Covenant Maker

The idea of God as *Covenant Maker* comes from the phrase "your God" (Exod. 20:2). God indeed is the Creator of the universe, but He isn't an impersonal superpower, force, or deity. He's a person who longs to have a personal and unique relationship with His people.

This is where the idea of marriage comes in. You've heard stories of friendships between a boy and girl where one or the other wants the friendship to develop into something deeper. Eventually, one of them gets up the nerve to say, "I love you."

The other casually responds, "I love you too." And the one who wants to take the relationship in a more intimate direction says, "No, really, I *love you!*" The other now clues in on what the other is saying and is faced with a choice. He or she can say, "*I love you too!*" or, "I love you, but only as a friend."

God is saying to us, "Really, I *love you!*" He doesn't want to have a casual relationship with us, where we only hang out with Him for an hour or so on Sunday mornings. He wants to become the most important and most intimate person in our lives day in and day out. He desires a unique relationship with us, where everything we do, say, think, and feel revolves around Him. It's something akin to marriage, which is why my opening illustration about marriage has everything to do with the first commandment. God made a covenant with His people, Israel, when He brought them out of Egypt and met with them at Mount Sinai. He makes a covenant with us today when we commit our lives in faith to the Lord Jesus Christ.

Just as a bride and groom make a lifelong commitment to each other, verbalized in the exchanging of vows and symbolized in the exchanging of rings, so God pledges Himself to us. When we put our faith in Jesus, God gives the Holy Spirit to indwell us.

In 2 Corinthians 1:21–22, Paul wrote, "Now He who establishes us with you in Christ and anointed us is God, who also sealed us and gave us the Spirit in our hearts as a pledge." Not only does this verse show us the Trinity—Father (God), Son (Christ), and Holy Spirit—but it's also a wonderful statement of God's covenant vow to every believer. God established and anointed us in Christ, and He has sealed us by His Spirit. In the ancient Roman world, a seal indicated ownership, authentication, distinction, confirmation, and security. The Holy

Spirit serves as a "pledge," or down payment, of our eternal relationship with God. This phrase could also be translated as an "engagement ring," signifying the promise of when the Bridegroom, Jesus, will return one day to take His bride, the church, and celebrate the "marriage supper of the Lamb" (Rev. 19:9).

God Is Redeemer

God is not only the Creator and Covenant Maker, but He is also the *Redeemer*. We see this in the phrase "who brought you out of the land of Egypt, out of the house of slavery" (Exod. 20:2). Just as God saved the Israelites from slavery, so He saves us from the penalty and power of sin. That's the point Paul made in Colossians 1:13–14: "For He rescued us from the domain of darkness, and transferred us to the kingdom of His beloved Son, in whom we have redemption, the forgiveness of sins."

Because of God's great love for us, He sent His Son, Jesus, to fulfill the Old Testament law, thereby making Him the final and only spotless sacrifice for human sin. As Paul put it in 2 Corinthians 5:21, "He made Him who knew no sin to be sin on our behalf, so that we might become the righteousness of God in Him." And everyone who puts their faith and trust in Jesus receives God's grace and salvation. Salvation and the forgiveness of sins come only through faith in Jesus Christ.

When Peter and John stood before the Jewish rulers after healing a man born lame, Peter explained to them, "Let it be known to all of you and to all the people of Israel, that by the name of Jesus Christ the Nazarene, whom you crucified, whom God raised from the dead—by this name this man stands here before you in good health" (Acts 4:10). Peter then turned the issue from physical healing to spiritual healing by declaring, "And there is salvation in no one else; for there is no other name under heaven that has been given among men by which we must be saved" (v. 12).

Paul echoed Peter's words when he wrote, "God our Savior . . . desires all men to be saved and to come to the knowledge of the truth" (1 Tim. 2:3–4). What truth is that? Paul explained in verse 5: "For there is one God, and one mediator also between God and men, the man Christ Jesus." God is our Redeemer.

God Is Rewarder

God is also our *Rewarder.* We see this in His promise that instead of captivity, the Israelites would have long life "in the land which the LORD your God gives you" (Exod. 20:12), with God showing lovingkindness to those who loved Him and kept His commandments (v. 6). For believers today, the rewards of esteeming God alone are a clear conscience, the power to resist sinful temptations, and an ever-present help in the person of the Holy Spirit (Ps. 46:1), who comforts us in our grief, guides us in our confusion, and intercedes for us in our prayers. We also have the future rewards of crowns in heaven and life in the new heaven and new earth, where we'll live forever in the presence of God and where every tear will be wiped away because "there will no longer be any death . . . mourning, or crying, or pain" (Rev. 21:4).

The Commandment on Esteeming God Alone

The first commandment, "You shall have no other gods before Me" (Exod. 20:3), is not only the first command in order and priority but also the fundamental motivation to obey all the other commandments. This most basic commandment

31

establishes the proper posture we should have before God that makes us able to obey the other nine.

Let's look at each part of the first commandment so we can develop a greater appreciation of what this command says about God and why we should esteem Him alone.

"Shall Have"

Wedding vows often include the phrase "to have and to hold from this day forward." Have you ever really thought about what it means "to have" someone?

To have means to own or possess something or someone; you have an exclusive claim others cannot make. For example, I *have* a car that others have no right to drive without permission. I *have* a home that others have no right to enter without an invitation. When it comes to my marriage, I *have* Amy as a unique relationship that excludes all others from making a claim on her marital love and affection. The same is true for Amy. She *has* me as her own special relationship. That's what it means when a man and woman vow to each other before God "to have and to hold." They're promising each other that they no longer belong to themselves but belong to each other—and none other. Adultery is destructive because it breaks this unique bond and says, "I can *have* another person in a similar way that I *have* my spouse." But that's a lie. I can't *have* another woman in the same way I *have* Amy because the other wouldn't be my wife; she would be a pretender, a fraud.

In the same way, "to have" God is to place Him in an exclusive position in your life—to live for Him in faithful obedience and loyalty, expressed in worship, service, and reverence, which the Bible says is the essence of wisdom.[5]

The problem with the children of Israel wasn't that they abandoned God but that they added to God. This is why the Lord often referred to Israel as an adulterous wife.[6] God demanded, "Either you have Me exclusively or you don't have Me at all." You can't have a both/and marriage, at least not for long. Marriage is an either/or relationship. You wouldn't come home and introduce your lover to your spouse with the promise of spending as much time, attention, and affection on your spouse as you spend on your lover. And your spouse wouldn't be unreasonable if they became jealous and demanded that you keep your vows of forsaking all others, *having* and *holding* them only.

"No Other Gods before Me"

Israel's unfaithfulness had to do with the other gods they chose to esteem along with the Lord while they were slaves in Egypt. Through the ten plagues, the Lord showed His power over all those pretenders. The Egyptians believed the Nile was the bloodstream of Osiris, the god of life and death. But in the hands of the Lord, Osiris bled out when God turned the Nile into blood. Egyptians worshiped the frog-goddess Heqet, but the Lord made them sick of frogs when millions of them crawled out of the Nile and covered the streets, invaded fields, and infiltrated businesses and homes. And so it went through each plague, the Lord demonstrating His sovereignty over the false gods of Egypt.

In the ninth plague, that of darkness, the Lord demonstrated His rule over the sun god Ra, whom Pharaoh was said to embody. The darkness was so thick the Egyptians "did not see one another, nor did anyone rise from his place for three days." But in Goshen, where the Israelites lived, there was light (10:23). With the tenth and final plague, the death of the firstborn, the Lord showed Himself as supreme sovereign over Egypt's powerless gods.

The Israelites were leaving behind the gods of the Egyptians. But what lay ahead were other gods, just as weak-kneed as the Egyptian gods but perhaps more beguiling—and for three reasons. First, Israel had lived four hundred and thirty years in a land dominated by polytheism, the worship of many gods. Remembering to worship God alone could be a challenge, especially since they were on their way to another land dominated by polytheism.

Second, the gods of the Canaanites, who occupied the promised land, were more appealing than the gods of Egypt. The worship of the Canaanite gods involved activities such as gluttony, drunkenness, and sex with temple prostitutes.[7]

Third, Israel tended to practice their faith as a both/and proposition, thereby diluting their esteem for the Lord with a dual allegiance. "The repeated refrain on idolatry throughout Israel's history will not be that she ceases worship of God *entirely*," Bible teacher Jen Wilkin wrote, "but that she ceases worship of God *alone*."[8]

Neither the gods of Egypt nor the gods of Canaan were a threat to the Lord. Like the one ring of power in the *Lord of the Rings*—"One Ring to rule them all"[9]—so there is one God to topple them all. But the Israelites needed to be careful "to have no other gods before [the Lord]." That is, they should esteem no gods but God alone.

Of course this wasn't just for Israel. Christians today can have "other gods," such as money, sex, and status. These false gods are described in 1 John 2:16 as "the lust of the flesh and the lust of the eyes and the boastful pride of life."

The Uniqueness of God

At its heart, the first commandment is about the uniqueness of God. The dictionary defines *unique* as "being the only one, without like or equal."[10] In other words, God is singular, unequaled, and distinctive. There is none like Him.

You may remember the Walt Disney animated films about Winnie the Pooh and his friends. One of the characters was Tigger, who sang a theme song about how wonderful Tiggers were. They were wonderful because their "tops were made out of rubber" and their "bottoms were made out of springs." But the most wonderful thing about Tiggers, as he sang, was that "I-I-I'm the only one."[11] God could sing that last line.

The uniqueness of God doesn't just mean there is none like Him but *there is none other than Him*. He isn't the supreme God among a pantheon of gods, greater than Zeus and Jupiter, or Ra and Osiris. Rather, He is the *one* and *only* God.[12] He is singular and exclusive. Zeus and Jupiter have never existed. Jen Wilkin was correct when she observed, "By commanding a singular allegiance, God does not merely assert that he is superior to other gods. Nor, in the plagues, does he merely demonstrate that he is stronger than other gods. He declares that they do not exist. They are nothing more than the vain imaginings of a darkened mind. The first word [commandment] is more than a prohibition against worshiping lesser gods; it is an invitation into reality. . . . Why should Israel worship no other gods before God? Because there are no other gods."[13]

Paul made this point clear in 1 Corinthians 8:4–6: "Some people say, quite rightly, that idols have no actual existence, that there's nothing to them, that there is no God other than our one God, that no matter how many of these so-called gods are named and worshiped they still don't add up to anything but a tall story. They say—again, quite rightly—that there is only one God the Father, that everything comes from him, and that he wants us to live for him. Also, they say that there is only one Master—Jesus the Messiah—and that everything is for his sake, including us. Yes. It's true" (MSG).

The great statement of Judaism, the Shema, declares the singularity and uniqueness of God: "Hear, O Israel! The LORD is our God, the LORD is one!" (Deut. 6:4). And because He is the one and only God, the Israelites (and we) were to love Him with their whole being (v. 5), teach their children daily about Him (vv. 6–7), obey Him (vv. 8–9), remember Him (vv. 10–12), and fear and worship Him (vv. 13–15). In short, they (and we) were to esteem Him alone.[14]

How to Esteem God in Our Lives

How can we can apply the first commandment to esteem God alone in our everyday lives?

First, *praise God the highest*. You may compliment the attractiveness of your spouse, the accomplishments of your children, and the loyalty of your friends, but who receives your greatest adoration? God should receive your highest praise.

Second, *depend on God first*. God likes to work through people and means, such as doctors, prescription drugs, employers, the kindness of friends and strangers, and family members. But when you're really in need, when your back is against the wall, where do you go? God should be the first one you turn to when you need help.

Third, *pray to God alone*. When you're looking for answers to life's difficulties, whom do you call? When you're overjoyed at good news, whom do you tell? When your heart is broken, to whom do you cry out? Do you turn to food or entertainment or work when your spirit is in need, feeling lonely, or wants to express gratitude, or do you turn to God with your invocation? It's good to talk about your problems and feelings with your friends and loved ones. But you should pray to God about everything as well. God always has what you need most, and He'll always be with you through anything.

Fourth, *thank God the most*. Who made sunny days, cool breezes, and the stars that glitter at night? Who gave you your skills and personality? Who sent His one and only Son to save you? God did that and so much more. He deserves your biggest and best thanks.

There's only room for one on the throne of your life. Who occupies it? I hope and pray it is God alone, who alone deserves your esteem.

2

The Second Commandment: Worship God Only

You shall not make for yourself an idol, or any likeness of what is in heaven above or on the earth beneath or in the water under the earth. You shall not worship them or serve them; for I, the LORD your God, am a jealous God, visiting the iniquity of the fathers on the children, on the third and the fourth generations of those who hate Me, but showing lovingkindness to thousands, to those who love Me and keep My commandments.

Exodus 20:4–6

I've always been fascinated with history, especially history associated with places, such as battlefields and buildings. I have fond memories of when my father took me to San Antonio to visit the Alamo. As a child standing in front of that famous facade, I imagined what it must have felt like on that day to see thousands of Mexican soldiers scaling the walls of that old mission.

As an adult, I've had the honor of visiting the most famous house in America, the White House. I've walked through the East Room, where the first couple to occupy the house, John and Abigail Adams, hung laundry while the building was still under construction. I've walked the Cross Hall, where Abraham Lincoln must have paced in agony during the Civil War. And I've stood in the Oval Office, where presidents have made decisions that shaped the future of our nation.

Just as we like tangible expressions of history—things we can touch and places we can go—we also like tangible expressions of faith. This is why trips to Israel are popular with Christians, and it's one reason our church offers a tour to Israel almost every year. To sail on the lake Jesus walked on, to sit on the steps where Jesus taught, to pray near the spot where Jesus prayed in the garden of Gethsemane, to look across the Kidron Valley to see Jerusalem and think that one day on that same hill, the Mount of Olives, Jesus will descend as King of kings and Lord of lords somehow makes our faith seem more real. I've never read the Bible the same way since my first trip to Israel in 1980. Locations and events from the Bible that I had only read about for the first twenty-five years of my life suddenly moved from the realm of the mythical and theoretical to concrete truths on which I could build my life.

Our desire for a tangible expression of our faith is natural, but it's also dangerous. The danger is that the place can become more important than the God of the place. This was the case for many first-century Jews, who thought more of the temple of God than the God of the temple. That's one reason

Jesus warned His disciples, "Truly I say to you, not one stone here [in the temple] will be left upon another, which will not be torn down" (Matt. 24:2). Less than forty years later, in AD 70, the Roman army destroyed the temple. Today, if you visit Israel, you'll see the massive stones the Romans toppled from the temple mount, lying where they landed two thousand years ago.

As finite human beings, it's only natural to want a tangible expression of our faith: something we can touch, something we can feel, something we can see. And that explains why through the years Christian pilgrims have searched for relics of the faith, such as supposed pieces of the cross or the nails that supposedly were driven into Christ's hands. Every time I witness a well-meaning pilgrim turn their attention to relics, it breaks my heart because in their misguided devotion they're violating the second commandment against worshiping God falsely.

Two Commandments That Sound like One

In the previous chapter, we looked at the first commandment: "You shall have no other gods before Me" (Exod. 20:3). Remember, the Israelites were getting ready to enter Canaan, a land in which the people worshiped many gods. So God was saying, "Don't be tempted to worship those false gods. You are to esteem only Me." Why should we esteem only God? Because God alone is our Creator, our Covenant Maker, our Redeemer, and our Rewarder. And God alone is a dynamic presence in our everyday lives, unlike the static, false idols the Canaanites and others worshiped.

As we continue reading verses 4–6, we come to the second commandment. God said to Moses, "You shall not make for yourself an idol, or any likeness of what is in heaven above or on the earth beneath or in the water under the earth. You shall not worship them or serve them; for I, the LORD your God, am a jealous God, visiting the iniquity of the fathers on the children, on the third and the fourth generations of those who hate Me, but showing lovingkindness to thousands, to those who love Me and keep My commandments."

Some denominations combine Exodus 20:3–6 into one commandment against false worship—namely, against worshiping other gods in the form of idols. (They come up with ten commandments by separating the last commandment into two parts. They say "You shall not covet your neighbor's house" is the ninth commandment, and "You shall not covet your neighbor's wife" is the tenth commandment.) Why do these groups view Exodus 20:3–6 as one commandment? The second commandment (vv. 4–6) strikes at the heart of their worship, since many of their practices are built around worshiping relics, images of the true God.

But I think there's good reason to see two separate commandments in these verses. The first commandment—"You shall have no other gods before Me" (v. 3)—is concerned with *whom* we are to worship. It forbids us from worshiping a false god instead of worshiping the only true God. The second commandment—"You shall not make for yourself an idol" (vv. 4–6)—is concerned with *how* we are to worship. Specifically, it tells us we shouldn't worship God with the aid of man-made images that could turn into idols.

The second commandment forbids us from making and worshiping a visible image of God. However, it doesn't prohibit the creation of art or aesthetic considerations. If it did, God would've violated His own commandment when He gifted

Bezalel and Oholiab as skilled craftsmen "to make artistic designs . . . in gold, in sliver, and in bronze, and in the cutting of stones . . . and in the carving of wood" (Exod. 31:4–5). These men adorned God's tabernacle with artistic representations of angels and palm trees, and they cast golden cherubim to sit on the lid of the ark of the covenant. God doesn't prohibit artistic endeavors. As one commentator put it, "What [God] prohibits is infusing any object with spiritual efficacy, as if man-made artifacts can bring us closer to God, represent God, or establish communion with God."[1]

Worship God Only

Just as we are to esteem God alone (the first commandment) and set Him as the top priority in our lives and to value Him above all others, so we are to worship God only (the second commandment). Like most of the Ten Commandments, the second commandment is stated negatively. The Lord outlined false ways to worship, as well as the punishment for disobedience. But He quickly turned the tables and gave us a positive motive for worshiping Him truly.

False Ways to Worship

The Israelites had just left a land of idolatry in Egypt and were on their way to a land of idolatry in Canaan, so naturally the Lord warned them against idolatry. He said, "You shall not make for yourself an idol, or any likeness of what is in heaven above or on the earth beneath or in the water under the earth. You shall not worship them or serve them" (Exod. 20:4–5).

Idolatry is loving and worshiping anything or anyone more than you love and worship God. That's not news to anyone who's familiar with the Bible. The Bible is filled with idol worshipers—some were pagans and some were supposedly faithful Jews. However, idolatry is more than the worship of false gods; it also involves the worship of the true God in a false way. And that's what the second commandment prohibits.

Specifically, the commandment forbids creating images or likenesses to represent God, as well as creating images or likenesses of heavenly, earthly, or sea creatures *as objects of worship and service*. That last phrase is important because, as I mentioned earlier, the painting of pictures or the carving of statues isn't prohibited. The command is against viewing these images as spiritually significant and necessary in our worship of God.

What's Wrong with Images of God?

These are reasons enough for God's prohibiting the creation of images that might become objects of worship or considered necessary to help us worship. But there are two other reasons that God prohibits making images.

Images Diminish the Glory of God

First, *images diminish the glory of God*. I love the story of the first grader in Sunday school who was busy at work with a crayon and paper. His teacher asked, "Johnny, what are you doing?" Johnny looked up and said, "I'm drawing a picture of God." His teacher said, "Well, nobody knows what God looks like." Johnny didn't miss a beat: "They will when I get finished."

It's a cute story, but the fact is nobody knows what God looks like, and any attempt to make a representation of God cannot help but reduce the majesty of God. It's impossible to capture the glory of God in any physical form. Anytime we try to make an image of God, we reduce God's glory. No image can accurately represent the totality of who God is.

But that didn't keep the Israelites from trying. They had followed an invisible God into the desert, and though He had provided proof of His presence through a pillar of cloud by day and a pillar of fire by night (Exod. 13:22), they wanted a visible representation of Him, especially after Moses disappeared in the cloud that covered the top of Mount Sinai. Fearing something terrible had happened to Moses because he didn't come down immediately, the people persuaded Aaron, Moses's brother, to forge a golden bull-calf—"a god who will go before us" (32:1). Aaron, who had seen firsthand the glory of the invisible God at work, agreed to do so. He said to them, "Tear off the gold rings which are in the ears of your wives, your sons, and your daughters, and bring them to me" (v. 2). Then Aaron "fashioned [the gold] . . . into a molten calf" (v. 4). When the people saw it, they worshiped it: "This is your god, O Israel, who brought you up from the land of Egypt" (v. 4).

Now, I want you to understand something here. Aaron was a godly man. He hadn't suddenly become a convert of Baal and decided to create a false god. When Aaron made this representation of a bull, he wasn't trying to get the people to worship a false god. He was trying to turn the hearts of the people toward the true God. He was saying, "Let's make this bull as a tangible representation of the God we believe in." Aaron violated the second commandment not because he created a depiction of a false god but because he created a *false depiction* of the true God.

How do I know this? In verse 5, Aaron issued a proclamation: "Tomorrow shall be a feast *to the* Lord." Aaron hadn't abandoned his faith in God. Rather, since the people struggled to believe in a God they couldn't see, Aaron attempted to bolster their faith by forging an animal that in Egypt represented divine power. The golden bull-calf was to symbolize God's strength—to give the people a visible and tangible representation of the invisible and intangible God they followed.

The problem with this image wasn't what it represented. Yes, God is a powerful God. That's true. But God is also a holy God. And He's a just God. And there are many other qualities of God that the bull couldn't represent. You see, the problem with any kind of image we make of God isn't that it necessarily communicates a false truth about God; it's that it doesn't communicate *all* the truth about God. Unfortunately, Aaron's false image of the true God resulted in worshiping Him in a false way. Aaron's intention was right, but his action was wrong—terribly wrong—because the golden calf diminished the true glory of God.

Incidentally, that's also true about a crucifix. What's wrong with an image of Christ on the cross? Well, it tells a truth about Jesus. It tells the truth that Jesus came and bled and died for our sins. And that's a wonderful truth. But that's not all the truth. The crucifix doesn't represent the power of Christ in rising from the dead three days later. It only tells one part of the story of Christ. And it's very easy for people to look at that image of Christ on the cross and descend into a morose mentality where they start thinking about their own suffering and wondering if Jesus identifies with their pain and the problems they're going through. And they soon miss the whole point of the cross. The point of the cross isn't only that Christ died but also that He rose again!

You might be wondering, "Pastor, aren't you being picky about that? I mean, how can a symbol tell all the truth about God?" Precisely. No image can tell all the truth about God, and that's why we're to refrain from using images as a means of worship.[2] Whenever you reduce the glory of God to an image, the result is going to be disappointment. That's why God's Word says we need to refrain from using images as objects of worship or as spiritual aids to worship.

The prophet Isaiah asked, "To whom then will you liken God? Or what likeness will you compare with Him?" (Isa. 40:18). The answer is no one and nothing. It's absurd to think we can create an image of the invisible God to help us worship Him. Don't diminish God's glory.

Images Distort the Truth about God

Second, *images distort the truth about God.* Aside from the desire to have tangible objects to reinforce our faith, some people feel compelled to reduce God to an image or statue so that God becomes more manageable to them. And that's why superstition often accompanies idolatry. When we reduce God to an image, we think then we can exercise control over that image and somehow control our own destiny. We can impose on that image whom we think God ought to be.

We see this in Romans 1, where Paul described the downward spiral of those who refuse to obey the first commandment to esteem God alone. He said, "Professing to be wise, they became fools, and exchanged the glory of the incorruptible God for an image in the form of corruptible man and of birds and four-footed animals and crawling creatures. Therefore God gave them over in the lusts of their hearts to impurity, so that their bodies would be dishonored among them. For

47

they exchanged the truth of God for a lie, and worshiped and served the creature rather than the Creator, who is blessed forever. Amen" (vv. 22–25).

Did you see a progression here? First, the people reduced God to something tangible—a statue in the form of a man or an animal. After they did that, they imposed their ideas of what God should be—in this case, a god of sexual promiscuity. They said, "That's what God is," and distorted the truth about God. That's the danger of images. Whenever we downsize God, we cannot help but then change God to become what we want Him to become.

By the way, this tendency to reduce God and then distort Him continues today. We see this illustrated in the movie *Evan Almighty*, a riff on the flood story in the Bible. In the film, Morgan Freeman plays "God" and comedian Steve Carell plays Evan Baxter, a businessman who becomes a modern-day Noah. "God" comes to Evan and tells him to build an ark because a flood is coming, just as in the days of Noah.

In a key scene in the movie, Evan asks "God" about the flood during Noah's time. And this is what God in the person of Morgan Freeman says: "You know, a lot of people miss the point of that story. They think it's about God's wrath and anger." Evan asks, "What is the story about, then? The ark?" And "God" answers, "Well, I think it's a love story about believing in each other. You know, the animals showed up in pairs. They stood by each other, side by side, just like Noah and his family. Everybody entered the ark side by side."[3]

Millions of people around the world saw that scene and thought, *Boy, isn't that great? Amen. That's the kind of God I want to worship.* Whenever we reduce God to an image, we distort Him to become the kind of god we want Him to become.

That's the Hollywood image of God—a god who judges no one and accepts everyone. We don't want a God of judgment and wrath. You can't control or manipulate that kind of God. But a "God" like Morgan Freeman, who offers easy answers to tough questions about the flood—who wouldn't want a god like that?

Somebody has said that in the beginning God created humans in His own image, and since that time humanity has been trying to repay the favor. We try to make God in our image. We want Him to be what we want Him to be.

By the way, anytime you hear somebody say, "When I imagine God, I imagine Him to be . . ." that's breaking the second commandment. That's an attempt to reduce God to your image of Him. The second commandment is also being broken whenever somebody says, "I could never worship a God who judges people based on their sexuality. I could never worship a God who sends people to hell just because they didn't believe the right things. I could never worship a God who allows suffering in the world when He has the power to stop it." Even today, people try to make God in their own image. And that's the basis of the second commandment. Don't diminish the glory of God, and don't distort the truth about God.

Motives to Worship Truly

Now that we've gained a better understanding of what it means to worship the true God in a false way, we need to understand the consequences of doing so. The Lord warned of His judgment if we disobey the second commandment. However, He also promised to be generous to those who worship Him truly. Both God's warning and His promise serve as motives for true worship.

He Is a Jealous God

To those who worship God falsely, He made His judgment clear: "I, the LORD your God, am a jealous God, visiting the iniquity of the fathers on the children, on the third and the fourth generations of those who hate Me" (Exod. 20:5). God is zealous in protecting His glory, which is diminished when images are used in worship. In Isaiah 42:8, God said, "I am the LORD, that is My name; I will not give My glory to another, nor My praise to graven images." God won't allow those who diminish His glory or distort the truth about Him to go unpunished. He will stand up for His great name by judging those who "hate" Him, which they demonstrate by disobeying His commandments.[4]

But what does God mean by "visiting the iniquity . . . on the third and fourth generations"?[5] Here's what it *doesn't* mean: God doesn't curse future generations because of someone's sin. A righteous child isn't punished for a wicked parent's sins. Ezekiel 18:20 makes this clear: "The person who sins will die. The son will not bear the punishment for the father's iniquity, nor will the father bear the punishment for the son's iniquity; the righteousness of the righteous will be upon himself, and the wickedness of the wicked will be upon himself."[6] Everyone is responsible for his or her own sin, just as everyone will be rewarded for his or her own righteousness.

So what *does* the warning in Exodus 20:5 mean? It concerns God's judgment on those who follow in the same sin of their parents, grandparents, and great-grandparents, disobeying the second commandment specifically but all of God's commandments generally. If you turn away from your ancestors' sins, then God will forgive and bless. But if you refuse to turn away from your ancestors' sins, then God will judge.

No one can point to their upbringing, cultural surroundings, or personal history to excuse disobedience. God deals with each generation as it comes, and He judges each generation if they choose to follow in the same disobedience as previous generations.

He Is a Generous God

There's a counterpoint to God's warning: "showing lovingkindness to thousands, to those who love Me and keep My commandments" (Exod. 20:6). God promises blessings for those who love Him and keep His commandments—to thousands of generations. Every individual in each new generation has a choice: hate God and disobey His commandments, or love God and obey His commandments. The first choice brings judgment; the second brings lovingkindness.

When the generation of Israelites who first received the Ten Commandments chose to disobey, the Lord punished them by making them wander in the desert for forty years (Num. 14:34). All but a few died. When the second generation arrived at the border of the promised land, Moses said, "I have set before you life and death, the blessing and the curse. So choose life in order that you may live, you and your descendants, by loving the LORD your God, by obeying His voice, and by holding fast to Him; for this is your life and the length of your days, that you may live in the land which the LORD swore to your fathers, to Abraham, Isaac, and Jacob, to give them" (Deut. 30:19–20).

How *Not* to Worship God

You might be thinking, *Pastor, I may have trouble with the other commandments, but this is one I'm not guilty of. I haven't made a graven image lately. I don't worship statues. I don't know how this applies to me.*

Can I suggest to you some ways we can apply this commandment? The second commandment says: don't downsize God. And there are three ways that all of us from time to time can be guilty of downsizing God.

Don't Diminish God through Images of Worship

We can diminish the glory of God through images of worship. Now, this is the most obvious application of this commandment. To use any kind of image as a means or an aid to worship is prohibited in the second commandment.

In most churches, and for most Christians, there is no more powerful image than the cross. Today, we get teary-eyed when we sing about the old rugged cross. But do you realize that the cross was not a symbol of worship for the first four hundred years of church history? In those days, the cross was a sign of the most horrible method of execution known. Nobody would think of using a cross as a symbol to worship. That would be like us going around today wearing an image of an electric chair. You wouldn't do that. It's a horrible symbol. It was only after the first four hundred years of church history that people started using the symbol of the cross as a means of worship.

I've known people who use these symbols as talismans—as good-luck charms—whenever they encounter difficulties. They hold these objects when they pray, pleading for God to rescue them from their troubles. There's nothing wrong with pleading to God, and there's nothing inherently wrong with displaying or wearing a cross. But when holding the object becomes entwined with an act of worship or prayer, then you've crossed the line and violated the second commandment.

Now the problem with images, like a cross, is that images appeal to the sensual rather than to the spiritual. This causes some Christians to confuse sentimentality with spirituality. The two are vastly different. For example, anytime I see the movie *Old Yeller*, I get misty-eyed. When I hear "The Star-Spangled Banner," I get a lump in my throat. But neither of those is spirituality. They're sentimentality.

A lot of Christians have reduced their faith to how they feel. After a church service, they'll say, "I just didn't feel anything today." Or they'll say, "I felt great!" How you feel isn't the issue in worship. It's how you act. It's what you do after worship that is the real measure of worship.

Can I give you a definition of *worship*? True worship occurs when a child of God, having heard the Word of God, submits to the Spirit of God in order to obey the will of God. That's the kind of worship God likes. When it comes to worship, your feelings count little with God; what counts with Him is what you do. Do you obey Him or not? Images of worship don't appeal to that which is spiritual. They appeal to that which is sentimental.

Don't Define God by Traditions of Worship

We can distort the truth about God when we define God by traditions of worship. I know a pastor who went to a century-old church. When he arrived, the first thing he did was remove the historic pulpit. That sent the congregation into a tizzy. They believed God couldn't speak unless the sermon was delivered from behind that pulpit. Their spiritual calculation led to the wrong conclusion: if you remove the pulpit, then you remove the authority of God's Word.

The tradition of the pulpit reaches back to Nehemiah 8:4, when Ezra "stood at a wooden podium which they had made for the purpose" and delivered the Word of God. Unfortunately, many churches see this passage as prescriptive, not descriptive, making us no better than the Pharisees, who "invalidated the word of God for the sake of [their] tradition" (Matt. 15:6). The Pharisees came up with so many rules and regulations that it was impossible for anyone to follow them all. Make sure you don't reduce God's glory to the traditions of worship. If we define God by our traditions, saying that God can only work in this way or that, then we violate the second commandment.

Don't Downsize God by Means of Worship

Another way we can be guilty of downsizing God is when we define God by the means of worship. God gave us different methods by which we might connect and communicate with Him: prayer, music, preaching, Bible reading, and the fellowship of the church. But these activities are means to an end, not an end in themselves. Never confuse God with music or prayer or preaching.

We are all drawn to certain styles in music or preaching, which can tempt us to assume God's blessing on one style over another. For example, at First Baptist Dallas, we have a wonderful music ministry, mixing traditional hymns with contemporary music because we believe God communicates through different types of music. Some churches have split because there was a change in the musical style. That's idolatry. To say God can't minister through contemporary music is to reduce the glory of God to notes on a page. The same is true for those who think they can't worship while singing hymns accompanied by a pipe organ and choir. Nonsense. God is more than musical choices. "How Great Thou Art" and "How Great Is Our God" are both wonderful expressions of God's glory, and neither should be looked down upon.

The same goes for the fellowship of the church. I've been in church ministry for a long time, and I can tell you that many people are more concerned about the reputation of their church than they are about the Head of their church. To hear some folks praise their pastor, you'd think their pastor was the Son of God instead of Jesus Christ. Now, the church is an important way we connect to God. It is impossible to be a growing Christian without being actively involved in a local church. But you can be actively involved in a local church and not be a growing Christian. And when you talk to some Christians about their relationship with God, they immediately start talking about their church involvement. But church involvement isn't the end; it's the means by which we connect to God. Be careful in glorifying the church over Christ, who established and is Lord of the church.

Finally, sometimes if we aren't careful we can even make an idol out of the Bible. There's no better way to know God than through His Word. The Bible is God's perfect revelation to us. But the goal of reading the Bible isn't to know about the Bible; it's to know the God of the Bible. The Bible is the means by which we learn about God and what He desires for our lives. There are people who love Bible knowledge and argue about doctrine—and they act just like unbelievers. That isn't worship. The goal of Bible study is to get us in touch with the Creator. We need to be careful that we don't reduce the God we are worshiping to the means of worship itself.

How *to* Worship God

In John 4:24, Jesus said, "God is spirit, and those who worship Him must worship in spirit and truth." In this verse, Jesus was saying three things. First, God is spirit—that is, He cannot be worshiped through tangible means. Second, God has to be worshiped in truth, not worshiped or defined by our own prejudices and traditions. Third, we need to make sure we're worshiping the true God, not some shadow of God that is found in music or in the church or even in the Bible itself. God is spirit, and those who worship Him must do so in spirit and in truth.

True spiritual worship is Christ-centered. It is Jesus who shows us the Father in all His glory (John 14:9). To look on Christ is to see the face of the one who couldn't be seen on Sinai. That's the mystery and the majesty of the incarnation. We don't make or worship images because we have the only image we'll ever need: Jesus Christ, who is the icon (*eikon*)— the image—of the invisible God (Col. 1:15). True worship occurs when we submit to the Spirit of God in order to do the will of God. This is the worship that fulfills the second commandment.

3

The Third Commandment: Revere God's Name

You shall not take the name of the LORD your God in vain, for the LORD will not leave him unpunished who takes His name in vain.

Exodus 20:7

A number of years ago, a Maryland man by the name of Irving West attended a high school carnival and got into a fight. A police officer working security broke it up and seized Mr. West, who proceeded to curse the officer with various profanities, including a particular expletive invoking God's condemnation. The next day, Mr. West appeared before the magistrate, who sentenced him to thirty days in jail and a twenty-five-dollar fine—the maximum for disorderly conduct. That wasn't a surprise. But what came next caught Mr. West off guard. The magistrate also sentenced him to an additional thirty days in jail and an additional fine for violating Maryland's blasphemy law, saying that Mr. West "did unlawfully use profanity by taking the Lord's name in vain in a public place."[1]

Mr. West got off easy because the Maryland statute said anyone who "shall write or utter any profane words of and concerning our Saviour, Jesus Christ . . . the Trinity . . . shall, on conviction, be fined not more than one hundred dollars, or imprisoned not more than six months, or both . . . at the discretion of the court."[2]

Mr. West was fortunate he didn't live during Old Testament days. God had a zero tolerance policy when it came to blaspheming His name. One strike and you're out. And though God doesn't deal with us like that today, He still takes seriously the third commandment: "You shall not take the name of the LORD your God in vain, for the LORD will not leave him unpunished who takes His name in vain" (Exod. 20:7).

Bible commentator Eugene Merrill paraphrased the third commandment this way: "You shall not lift up the name of Yahweh your God without reason."[3] That's what this commandment is talking about. It prohibits not just using the name of God in profanity but also needlessly invoking the name of God, whether it be in jest or in anger. God's name is sacred, and it's to be treated that way.

What's in a Name?

Shakespeare made famous the statement, "What's in a name? That which we call a rose by any other name would smell as sweet."[4] It's a good question. What's in a name that makes it so important?

Why did your parents give you your name? Do you know what your name means? Mine means "bright fame," "brilliant," or "bringer of light."[5] I can tell you there's nothing brilliant about me, but "bringer of light" is appropriate since I preach the "Light of the world" to those in spiritual darkness so they might have the "Light of life" (John 8:12).

Expectant parents often name their children after relatives or historical figures, follow popular trends, or consider how a first name sounds with the family's last name. Other times, parents decide to name a yet-unborn child after someone beloved and admired, hoping they will live up to their namesake. Amy and I named our first daughter, Julia, after my mother, praying that she would be the same powerful witness for Christ her grandmother was—and Julia has been. Our second daughter was named after my grandmother Dorothy, who was known for her kindness and humor, and our Dorothy mirrors both characteristics without ever having met her great-grandmother. We based our children's names on our hopes of what they would become.

But that's not how expectant parents during biblical days named their children. They might give a son a father's or grandfather's name, but often parents picked names based on circumstances at the time of birth, such as Jacob, who was given a name meaning "heel grabber" because he held on to the heel of his twin brother, Esau, at birth (Gen. 25:26). Jabez's mother must have experienced a painful event around the time of his birth, because she named him "pain" (1 Chron. 4:9–10). Other parents named their children based on character traits they observed in their children. The seeds of foolishness must have been present in Nabal at an early age, since his name means "fool" (1 Sam. 25:25). Joshua's parents, who had been born into slavery, hoped their son might see the salvation of the Lord—and he did. Not only did Joshua experience miraculous freedom from Egyptian bondage but he was a leading participant in God's plan to bless His people. The name Joshua means "Yahweh is salvation," and it's the root of the name Jesus.

Whenever we encounter a name in the Bible, it tells us something about the character of the individual. This is also true of God's names. When we read "the name of the LORD," as we do in Exodus 20:7, we can substitute it with "the character of the LORD" because God's name represents the totality of His character.

God Shows Himself by Speaking His Name

The third commandment's prohibition against using God's name in vain can be applied to all His names and titles, but it specifically addresses God's personal name. You might be thinking, *I don't see God's name in Exodus 20:7. I see the title "LORD," but I don't see a personal name.* The title is the name. The translators of our English Bibles depict God's personal name as the title "Lord" written in small caps: LORD. This follows the Hebrew tradition of not writing God's name because of its holiness.

So what is God's personal name, the one represented as "LORD" in Exodus 20:7? The name that is used here is the most holy, sacred name of God: Yahweh. It's a Hebrew word translated "to be." It's the name God used when He identified himself to Moses in the burning bush: "I AM WHO I AM" (3:14).

God told Moses in verse 15 that His name is personal, relational, and covenantal: "Thus you shall say . . . 'The LORD

[Yahweh], the God of your fathers, the God of Abraham, the God of Isaac, and the God of Jacob, has sent me to you.' This is My name forever, and this is My memorial-name to all generations."

Later in Exodus, Moses asked God to *show* him His glory. God's response was to *speak* His name: "I Myself will make all My goodness pass before you, and will proclaim the name of the LORD [Yahweh] before you" (33:19). God did just that in chapter 34: "Then the LORD passed by in front of [Moses] and proclaimed, 'The LORD, the LORD God, compassionate and gracious, slow to anger, and abounding in lovingkindness and truth; who keeps lovingkindness for thousands, who forgives iniquity, transgression and sin; yet He will by no means leave the guilty unpunished, visiting the iniquity of fathers on the children and on the grandchildren to the third and fourth generations'" (vv. 6–7).[6]

So holy was God's personal name, Yahweh, that it was not to be spoken in Israel.[7] It was simply referred to as "the Name." In fact, if you look at the name *Yahweh* in the Hebrew Old Testament, there are no vowels, only consonants. In the English alphabet, it looks like this: *YHWH*. There was no way to pronounce it. It was not to be uttered, so sacred was God's name.

God Takes the Holiness of His Name Seriously

Jewish scribes refused to commit God's name to paper, believing that writing God's sacred name with human hands would diminish its holiness. They knew God took the holiness of His name seriously.

Psalm 111:9 says, "Holy and awesome is His name." The Hebrew word translated "awesome" (*yare*) can also be translated as "worthy of reverence." It's linked to the idea of fear in verse 10: "The fear of the LORD is the beginning of wisdom." This type of fear is reverential awe of God's person, His character, and His name. It's a healthy fear that comes from recognizing who we are in relation to who God is. God is holy, and we are unholy; therefore, we should uphold the name of God with all due respect, honor, and glory. God alone is worthy of our reverence—and that is what the writer of the psalm was getting at and what the third commandment demands.

An episode in Leviticus 24 illustrates just how seriously the Lord takes His name and this third commandment, particularly the last half: "the LORD will not leave him unpunished who takes His name in vain" (Exod. 20:7). The incident involves an unnamed man who got into a fight and, during the scuffle, insulted and cursed his opponent (Lev. 24:10).[8] In the heat of the moment, he also "blasphemed the Name" (v. 11)—that is, he cursed God, either directly or by using God's name in a curse directed at his opponent (as Mr. West did). When the witnesses of the fight heard the man curse God, they intervened and brought the man to Moses for judgment (vv. 11–12). "The LORD spoke to Moses, saying, 'Bring the one who has cursed outside the camp, and let all who heard him lay their hands on his head'" (vv. 13–14). The instruction for the witnesses to lay their hands on the offender's head was a symbolic act of transference, a way for the witnesses to cleanse themselves from secondhand blasphemy and to signify that the blasphemer was responsible for his words.

Then the Lord passed judgment: "Let all the congregation stone him. . . . The one who blasphemes the name of the LORD shall surely be put to death" (vv. 14, 16). Fortunately, God doesn't punish us like that when we violate the third commandment. But that doesn't mean He no longer takes the holiness of His name seriously.

You may be thinking, *That's the Old Testament, Pastor. God lightened up in the New Testament. He doesn't take this nearly as seriously as that Old Testament God did. We don't serve a God of wrath; we serve a God of love.* Have you ever heard that before? The Bible says God is "the same yesterday and today and forever" (Heb. 13:8). We see the holiness of God's name in the prayer of Jesus that we often call the Lord's Prayer.

In Matthew 6, Jesus taught His disciples how to pray. It's interesting when we look at this model prayer. What is the very first thing Jesus taught us to pray for? World peace? Feeding the hungry? The salvation of the lost? No. The very first thing in the Lord's Prayer is, "Our Father who is in heaven, hallowed [sacred, reverenced] be Your name" (v. 9). You see, to Jesus Christ, the holiness, the reverence, the reputation of God was above all. It was the priority in His life.

Why does God take the holiness of His name so seriously? As I said earlier, the name of God describes the person of God—the two are inseparably linked. Here's a simple illustration to show you what I mean. What do you think of when I say the name Abraham Lincoln? How about Adolf Hitler? For Lincoln, you might conjure up images of a bearded man with a careworn face, and for Hitler you might imagine a short man with a funny mustache. But then you think about their character—what they stood for, what they stood against, the kinds of words and actions they used in their lives. In other words, the name invokes the personhood—the intimate identity—of each man.

When you say someone's name, there's an image that comes to mind, positive or negative. The name represents the essence of that person. The same is true when we speak the name of God. It should always lead to the conclusion that the Lord is holy, loving, good, merciful, gracious, and the other attributes that make up His divine character.

Whenever we use the name of God in an irreverent way, we're in a sense reducing the glory of God. The third commandment flows out of the second commandment. The second commandment says, "Don't reduce God to an image. Don't diminish your thoughts about God." The third commandment says, "Don't dishonor God through your speech. Don't trivialize Him by the way you talk." And that's what happens when we use God's name needlessly, without reason. We reduce the majesty of God not only in our own minds but in the minds and the hearts of those around us.

I used to subscribe to a magazine called *Writer's Digest*. Since the magazine was a trade journal for writers, it wasn't unusual to see advertisements from manufacturers cautioning writers against misusing their company's name. For example, an ad warned writers not to say somebody grabbed a kleenex, with a lowercase *k*, to refer to a tissue of any brand. They said writers who use their brand name should treat it as a proper name and capitalize it. Similarly, writers shouldn't use the brand name Coke (for the soft drink Coca-Cola) as a stand-in for other soft drinks. It's a running joke in Texas that if you ask for a Coke, what you really mean is a Dr Pepper. Most of the ads from various companies would close with a statement like this: "We have spent millions of dollars to develop our name and establish that name with a product. Please don't destroy that work through carelessness, or you will face the consequences." Today, companies spend millions of dollars litigating the misuse of their names.

If companies will go to such great lengths to protect their names and reputations, then how much more will God protect His name and reputation? Whenever you use God's name in a flippant way, you denigrate His brand, so to speak. You reduce the glory of God in the minds of other people.

How Do We Take God's Name in Vain?

The first three commandments warn against something lowly or careless in relation to God. The first commandment deals with our *beliefs* about God; the second commandment concerns our *thoughts* about God; the third commandment involves our *words* about God. Beliefs determine thoughts, and thoughts determine words. And words determine whether we're taking God's name in vain.

On the surface, it seems we could avoid breaking the third commandment simply by not using profanity. But this isn't what the third commandment is prohibiting. It's a warning against taking God's name in vain, not a warning against profanity in general.[9]

The commandment says, "You shall not take the name of the LORD your God in vain" (Exod. 20:7). The phrase translated "take in vain" literally means "to lift up or attach to emptiness." The implication, as the New International Version translates the verse, is we are not to "*misuse* the name of the LORD [our] God." How might we misuse God's name by stripping it of honor, glory, and holiness? Let me suggest four broad categories.

Profanity

Profanity is the most obvious way in which people take God's name in vain. The word *profane* means to debase something holy, to bring it down to our level and reduce it to be nothing more than we are. Profanity in speech typically comes out of anger, like we saw with Mr. West and the blaspheming man of Leviticus 24, where others are damned in the name of God.

But it's not just outbursts of anger with God's name attached that are off-limits. So are outbursts of shock or outrage that invoke the name of God. How many times have you seen or heard on social media, or even used yourself, the acronym OMG—"Oh my God"? This phrase and acronym may be acceptable in our culture today, but it doesn't uphold the holiness of God's name. It debases His name by making it an expression of surprise or shock. The same goes for saying "God" or "Jesus Christ" as a way to convey outrage or in such a way that His name becomes a throwaway word.

Falsehoods

Falsehoods include lies, half-truths, and deceptions. Related to the third commandment, one of the most basic ways we profane God's name is when we invoke God's name to manipulate people to do what we want them to do.

It is taking God's name in vain to say God told you something that in fact He really didn't. For example, a teenager says to his parents, "God spoke to me in a dream and told me you were supposed to buy me a new car." Or an employer says to her employee, "I was intent on giving you a raise, but God told me this wasn't the year to do that." By the way, preachers can be the worst at using God's name to manipulate people by saying things like, "God told me we're supposed to build this building." We break the third commandment anytime we invoke God's name to get people to do what we want, essentially saying, "You better do what I've told you to do, because God told me."

As I look back on my life, there are only two times when I believed God spoke to my heart directly, and in each case it was about what I was supposed to do, not what somebody else was supposed to be doing. That's usually how God speaks. Make sure you don't use God's name to manipulate other people.

We also violate this commandment when we make promises and attach God's name to them, saying, "I swear to God" or "As God is my witness." Don't do that. If you do break your word, you've implicated God in your failure. Theologian J. I. Packer called that "monstrous irreverence."[10] Jesus said as much in Matthew 5: "Let your statement be, 'Yes, yes' or 'No, no'" (v. 37). James said the same (5:12).[11] The point is this: a believer's promise should be as trustworthy as those of God Himself and needs no extra oaths to make it so.

Here's another way we misuse God's name by falsehood: we accuse Him of things that aren't true, like blaming Him for our sin even though He doesn't tempt us to sin (1:13). This goes back to the garden of Eden. Adam said to God, "It was *the woman you gave me* who gave me the fruit, and I ate it" (Gen. 3:12 NLT). It was *the kids You gave me* that caused me to become angry. It was *the job You gave me* that caused me to become greedy. It was *the spouse You gave me* that caused me to fall into pornography and adultery. All Adam needed to say was, "I ate it."

Whenever we fail to tell the truth and attach God's name to it, we've broken the third commandment.

Frivolity

We also violate the third commandment when we use God's name in a careless or trivial manner, such as telling jokes where

God the Father or Jesus Christ becomes the punchline. For example, we profane God's name in a joke that starts out with, "Did you hear the one about God talking to the rabbi and the priest and the Baptist preacher?" These attempts at humor aren't meant to be harmful, but they're using God's name in a flippant, irreverent way.

Call me old-fashioned, but I was taught that children didn't call their parents by their first names out of respect for them. We can call Jesus by His given name, but we must never forget that He isn't just one of the boys, any more than God the Father is "the Big Man Upstairs." Jesus is the Lord of heaven and earth, the Son of God, the Savior and Redeemer.

There's a scene in the movie *The American President* that reminds me not to treat Jesus or God's name lightly. Michael Douglas plays President Andrew Shepherd. His chief of staff is A. J. MacInerney, portrayed by Martin Sheen. They're shooting pool, discussing a personal matter, and though they've been lifelong friends, A. J. refuses to call the president by his first name. When Andrew sinks the ball, A. J. says, "Nice shot, Mr. President." "Nice shot, Mr. President?" Andrew says. "You won't even call me by my name when we're playing pool?" A. J. responds, "I will not do it playing pool, I will not do in a school. I do not like green eggs and ham, I do not like them, Sam I Am."[12]

Never trivialize the name of God.

Phoniness

Phoniness is hypocrisy. That's what Jesus called it in Matthew 15:7. He said, "This people honors Me with their lips, but their heart is far away from Me" (v. 8). This plays out, in the words of one writer, when "we . . . misuse the name of the Lord by speaking hallowed words while living hollow lives."[13]

What does this look like practically? Here are some examples. Whenever the worship leader stands up on Sunday morning and sings praises to God but on Monday morning has no thought of God and engages in a habitual sin. Whenever a pastor prays with piety and preaches with eloquence on Sunday morning but on Monday morning doesn't pray or read the Bible. Whenever we're at church singing praises to God but our minds are on what we're having for lunch or on the football game that afternoon. Whenever parents demand that their children apologize for wrongdoing but refuse to apologize whenever they are in the wrong.

No wonder Jesus asked of hypocrites, "Why do you call Me, 'Lord, Lord,' and do not do what I say?" (Luke 6:46). If your intention is to keep the third commandment, make sure you practice what you preach—or else keep your mouth shut.

Why Do We Take God's Name in Vain?

We've seen that God takes seriously the holiness of His name. Why would anyone violate a commandment that God takes so seriously? I can think of three reasons.[14]

A Lack of Knowledge

Some people aren't aware of the third commandment or don't understand its implications. There are some people who walk around saying "My God" all the time, not knowing that they're violating this command. Even though it's accepted in our culture, it's not acceptable to God. Some people just don't understand that. Perhaps you didn't before reading this chapter. Now you do. If you've unknowingly misused God's name in the past, then you know what to do now: stop it.

A Lack of Self-Control

There are some people who just can't seem to help themselves. They use God's name in vain so habitually that they can't stop. If this is you, let me suggest three principles to help you. First, *admit to God your need to control your speech.* Self-control is a fruit of the Spirit (Gal. 5:23). The inability to control your speech is evidence of a lack of being controlled by the Holy Spirit.

Second, *disassociate yourself from those who take God's name in vain on a regular basis.* Profanity is a learned response—more caught than taught. You've heard of parents whose children curse, and they are "surprised" as to where little Johnny or Janie learned such language. Proverbs 22:24–25 advises, "Do not associate with a man given to anger [whose outburst may cause him to damn God and others in God's name]; or go with a hot-tempered man, or you will learn his ways and find a snare for yourself."

Third, *fill your mind with edifying thoughts about God.* Remember, beliefs determine thoughts, and thoughts determine words. Proverbs 23:7 says, "As [a person] thinks within himself, so he is." Paul wrote, "Let no unwholesome word proceed from your mouth, but only such a word as is good for edification according to the need of the moment, so that it will give grace to those who hear" (Eph. 4:29).

A Lack of Genuine Salvation

I don't believe it's possible for a genuinely saved person, one who's come to grips with their sin and the sacrifice Christ made on their behalf, to habitually and repeatedly blaspheme the name of God or the Son of God. To do so is to betray the one who gave His life to save yours. For the genuine believer, the name of God the Father, Jesus the Son, and the Holy Spirit are sacred.

Imagine me officiating a funeral service and beginning by saying, "Hey, did you hear the joke about the undertaker who . . . ?" It would be inappropriate to make a joke about death as I looked at people who have come face-to-face with the sorrow of death. Or imagine me standing up at an Alcoholics Anonymous meeting and saying, "Hey, did you hear the one about the two drunks?" We would never joke about alcoholism in the face of those who had suffered its effects. In the same way, people who have come face-to-face with their own sin and then have come face-to-face with the grace of Jesus Christ, who gave His life for us, cannot repeatedly and habitually use His name in an irreverent way. I don't believe it's possible for a genuinely saved person to habitually and repeatedly blaspheme the name of Jesus Christ. To do so is to betray the lack of a genuine salvation experience.

For a believer, the name of Jesus is a sacred name. To the unbeliever, it's a name just like any other name. I saw that contrast years ago when I was invited to speak at an event hosted by a Christian university. When I finished speaking, the host of the event stood up and started talking, peppering his speech with God's name in jest—God this and God that and Lordy, Lordy this—and joking, "Those of you who didn't go to our university, you just need to bow your head right now and pray that God would cleanse you of your sin for not going," and on and on. It was nauseating to hear him use the name of God in that way. Then they invited a woman to come onto the platform to receive an award. She said, "Anything good in my life is because of what God has done for me. He's the one who saved me. He's the one who selected me for this service. He's the one to whom all glory and honor is due." Two people with two very different uses of the name of God.

If you have truly been saved, if you have truly experienced the grace of God in your life, it's going to be reflected in your speech. To a person who has been saved, the name of God is something to be reverenced.

How Can We Avoid Taking God's Name in Vain?

Let me close this chapter with a final word of encouragement and challenge. The way to avoid taking the name of God in vain is to take seriously Colossians 3:17: "Whatever you do in word or deed, do all in the name of the Lord Jesus, giving thanks through Him to God the Father."

We obey the third commandment by living Christianly, speaking the truth in love, putting away our sin, doing acts of service, placing others above ourselves, and praising Him wholeheartedly. When we do these things, and do them in Christ, for Christ, and through Christ, then we honor His name—"the name which is above every name," and at whose name "every knee will bow . . . [and] every tongue will confess that Jesus Christ is Lord, to the glory of God the Father" (Phil. 2:9–11).

4

The Fourth Commandment: Value God's Day

Remember the sabbath day, to keep it holy. Six days you shall labor and do all your work, but the seventh day is a sabbath of the LORD your God; in it you shall not do any work, you or your son or your daughter, your male or your female servant or your cattle or your sojourner who stays with you. For in six days the LORD made the heavens and the earth, the sea and all that is in them, and rested on the seventh day; therefore the LORD blessed the sabbath day and made it holy.

Exodus 20:8–11

We live in a harried and hurry-up culture. With smartphones in our pockets and purses, we're forever plugged in and available through email, text messages, and social media. But we weren't meant to go, go, go without end.

This reminds me of a story about a man who traveled to Africa. To ensure he could travel at a speedy pace, he hired a guide and a couple of local tribesmen to carry his luggage and do whatever was needed. This traveler told his guide and porters, "We're going to get up before the sun rises and not stop until the sun sets." And boy, did they move that day. Faster and faster, the man prodded the guide and porters along.

The next morning, the traveler rose with the sun and found his helpers seated under a shade tree. He instructed the men to get moving. But the porters wouldn't move. Despite his repeated demands, the men sat in silence. Finally, the traveler asked the guide, "What's the matter with these men?"

The guide explained, "You've pushed them so hard and so fast they are now waiting for their souls to catch up with their bodies."[1]

Fortunately, God designated one day out of every week when we can do just that. It's called the Sabbath—and it's the subject of the fourth commandment, which says, "Remember the sabbath day, to keep it holy. Six days you shall labor and do all your work, but the seventh day is a sabbath of the LORD your God; in it you shall not do any work, you or your son or your daughter, your male or your female servant or your cattle or your sojourner who stays with you. For in six days the LORD made the heavens and the earth, the sea and all that is in them, and rested on the seventh day; therefore the LORD blessed the sabbath day and made it holy" (Exod. 20:8–11).

This commandment says there's one day of each week in which we're to do no work. It's a day we set aside for worship and rest.

Observations about the Fourth Commandment

The fourth commandment is unique among the ten for at least three reasons. First, *more space is devoted to the fourth commandment than the others.* I think it's interesting that God had more to say about the Sabbath than He did about theft, adultery, or murder. It's also one of the most mentioned commandments in the Old Testament. Why is it significant that the Lord had so much to say about the Sabbath? It tells us that the fourth commandment isn't something we can keep only when we feel like it or can find the time.

This commandment isn't forgotten, certainly not in Israel. If you ever travel to Israel, make sure you pay attention to the day of the week and read carefully the signs posted on elevators, because if you forget it's a Saturday and get on the wrong elevator, you'll stop at every floor. The first time I accidentally boarded a Shabbat elevator I was aggravated at all the stops, assuming some mischievous child had pressed all the buttons! But rabbis have determined that pushing the button for your desired floor is considered work, violating the Sabbath. So Shabbat elevators are programmed to stop at every floor.

Second, *Jesus never repeated the fourth commandment.* This is the only one of the Ten Commandments Jesus didn't repeat directly, nor did the New Testament writers spend much time on it. Why? It's because the day changed. Jesus rose from the dead on the *first day* of the week, Sunday, so Christians set that day aside for worship as a memorial to Him.[2] Whether we worship on Saturday or Sunday, the idea of Sabbath is to make the day one of spiritual service through religious observance.

Third, *the fourth commandment is one of only two commandments stated positively.*[3] We often think of the Sabbath in the negative—about what we're *not* allowed to do on the Sabbath day. Do you remember blue laws? For many years, states had legal restrictions about what you were allowed to buy and do on Sundays.

I don't know how it was when you were growing up, but in the particular Baptist culture I grew up in, the most debauched thing you could do on a Sunday was to go to the movies. I remember my grandparents, who were Methodist, used to visit us for Sunday lunches. On occasion, after lunch, my grandmother would excuse herself and go to the movies. I never wanted to be a Methodist so bad in my life than on those Sunday afternoons when my grandmother went to the movie theater! But there was no way my father or mother would allow me to accompany my grandmother on those Sunday afternoons.

Where did we come up with the idea that people couldn't go to the movies on a Sunday? In all honesty, we made it up. Do you know who else made up things out of thin air to promote the correct observance of the Sabbath? That's right—the Pharisees.

The Pharisees took this commandment and added all kinds of regulations about what people couldn't do on the Sabbath.[4] Jesus had an interesting take on that. He loved to turn the Pharisees' thoughts upside down and certainly did that when it came to the Sabbath.[5] Mark 2:23–28 says, "And it happened that He was passing through the grainfields on the Sabbath, and His disciples began to make their way along while picking the heads of grain. The Pharisees were saying to Him, 'Look, why are they doing what is not lawful on the Sabbath?' . . . Jesus said to them, 'The Sabbath was made for man, and not man for the Sabbath. So the Son of Man is Lord even of the Sabbath.'"

This is a key principle to understand when we try to apply this commandment. People were not made for the Sabbath; the Sabbath was God's gift to people. God gave the Sabbath day to us for our physical, emotional, and spiritual well-being.

Questions about the Fourth Commandment

Let's look at the particulars of the Sabbath commandment found in Exodus 20:8–11 by asking and answering four key questions.

What Is the Sabbath?

The word *sabbath* comes from the Hebrew word *shabbat,* literally meaning "cease," "stop," or "rest"—just as the Lord said: "Remember the *sabbath* day, to keep it holy. . . . For in six days the LORD made the heavens and the earth, the sea and all that is in them, and *rested* on the seventh day; therefore the LORD blessed the *sabbath* day and made it holy" (vv. 8, 11). The Israelites were to follow God's pattern of working six days and resting (or sabbathing) on the seventh day (Gen. 2:2–3; Exod. 16:23). For them that meant Saturday, since their week began on Sunday.

But why did God stop working after six days of creation? Did He wipe His brow and say, "Wow, that was a tough week! I'm exhausted. I think I'll take tomorrow off"? Did God need to put up His feet and rest because He was worn out? Did He run out of creative ideas? Hardly. God could've continued creating past the six days if He wanted to. So why did He stop? Why stop at whatever number of trees there are in the world? Why not create a billion more stars in the sky? I think God stopped because He created everything that needed to be created. In other words, there came a time when God said,

"That's enough." Or, as Moses concluded in Genesis 1, "God saw all that He had made, and behold, it was very good" (v. 31).

There's another reason God stopped working after six days: He wanted to establish a pattern for His image bearers to follow. God created the universe to operate on a set of rules—scientific principles, we might say. Twenty-four-hour days come from the earth's rotation on its axis, the movement of the moon basically determines our months, and a 365-day year is the result of the earth revolving around the sun. But a seven-day week isn't determined by any of those factors. In a sense, it's more theological than scientific because God chose to create the universe in six days and to rest on the seventh.

So, whenever we go through a Sunday-Monday-Tuesday-Wednesday-Thursday-Friday-Saturday cycle, God is reminding us that we should follow His lead. We should close our computers, put down our hammers, and take off our aprons and say, "That's enough for this week; I've done what needed doing. Now it's time to rest."

What Does It Mean to "Remember"?

The fourth commandment opens simply enough: "Remember the sabbath day, to keep it holy" (Exod. 20:8). But what does it mean to "remember"? Two things. First, to remember means to recall from memory. How could the Israelites recall this command from memory if this was the first time God gave the Ten Commandments? The Sabbath day was part of an earlier tradition.

During the time when the Hebrews gathered manna in the wilderness, the Lord instructed them to gather only enough to feed their families for that day—their "daily bread," as Jesus taught His disciples to pray (Matt. 6:11). On the sixth day, however, the people were to gather enough for *two* days. Here's what Moses intructed: "'Tomorrow is a sabbath observance, a holy sabbath to the LORD. Bake what you will bake and boil what you will boil, and all that is left over put aside to be kept until morning.' So they put it aside until [the seventh] morning, as Moses had ordered, and it did not become foul nor was there any worm in it. Moses said, 'Eat it today, for today is a sabbath to the LORD; today you will not find it in the field. Six days you shall gather it, but on the seventh day, the sabbath, there will be none'" (Exod. 16:22–26).

With the giving of the law in Exodus 20, the Sabbath became part of the Israelites' covenant relationship with God. The Lord didn't command Gentile nations to observe the seventh day as special (Ps. 147:19–20), so the Sabbath came to represent a unique sign between God and His people.[6]

Second, to remember means to memorialize through obedience. Since the seventh day is "holy" we ought to act accordingly—namely, ceasing from work and resting. To *remember* the Sabbath, then, is to *obey* the command.

What Does It Mean God "Blessed" and "Made Holy" the Sabbath?

God made the Sabbath day "holy" because He "blessed" it (Exod. 20:11), which is to say He set aside the seventh day as *special* and *different* from the other days of the week. The reasons God did this are found in the unique language attached to the command in Exodus 20 and Deuteronomy 5. In Exodus, the Lord instructed the people to remember the Sabbath day because it was rooted in *creation*: "For in six days the LORD made the heavens and the earth, the sea and all that is in them, and *rested* on the seventh day; therefore the

LORD blessed the sabbath day and made it holy" (20:11; Gen. 2:2–3). In Deuteronomy, the Lord instructed the people to remember the Sabbath day because it was rooted in *redemption*: "You shall remember that you were a slave in the land of Egypt, and the LORD your God brought you out of there by a mighty hand and by an outstretched arm; therefore the LORD your God commanded you to observe the sabbath day" (5:15; Exod. 6:6).

That's what it means for *God* to bless the Sabbath day and make it holy. But what does it mean for *us* to make the Sabbath day holy, as God commanded in Exodus 20:8? Well, it means much the same: to separate the seventh day (or for Christians, the first day, Sunday) from the other six days as a special day set aside for the Lord. Think of it like Thanksgiving, Christmas, or the Fourth of July. In our calendar, we set aside each of these days as unique and worthy of remembering or celebrating. The same is true for the Sabbath day, where one day a week is marked out as special unto the Lord.

Practically speaking, we make the Sabbath holy by obeying the command, "Six days you shall labor and do all your work, but the seventh day is a sabbath of the LORD your God; in it you shall not do any work" (vv. 9–10). So we set that day aside to focus our attention on the living Lord, for worship and well-being. It becomes a day of rest that reorients and restores.

What Was the Penalty for Violating the Sabbath?

Individuals who violated the Sabbath command during the Old Testament profaned God's day and were stoned to death (Exod. 31:15; Num. 15:32–36). Nationally, failure to obey a similar command to allow the land to lay fallow every seventh year (Lev. 26:34, 43) resulted in exile—one year for every seventh year of disobedience (seventy years of exile for 490 years of disobedience).

Fortunately, when we get to the New Testament and into the present day, the penalty for disobeying the fourth commandment isn't death or exile. In fact, there's no stated penalty ever since Christians shifted our day of worship to Sunday, the day when Jesus rose from the grave. We're free to choose which day to rest and worship without fear of punishment.

Practical Principles from the Fourth Commandment Today

Christians today aren't under the same obligation to obey the fourth commandment as the Israelites, because the death and resurrection of Christ altered the day set aside for worship and rest. But the principle (the spirit) of the fourth commandment is still in effect. We should designate a day to cease from our labors for the purpose of meeting together in corporate worship of our risen Savior.

I believe the fourth commandment affirms four principles that are just as practical for Christians today as they were for the Israelites then.

Human Dignity

The Sabbath affirms human dignity. Before the Lord issued the fourth commandment, human history was little more than unending toil, turning human beings into beasts of burden. But Exodus 20 changed all that by recognizing the inherent dignity in every person, transforming them from burden bearers to image bearers, insisting they cease working one day out of seven so they may worship the Lord, in whose image they are made.

The ancestors of the Israelites were slaves in Egypt, making mud bricks. They didn't get a day off; slaves weren't granted Sabbaths. The only rest they knew was the rest that came with death—until God rescued them, demonstrating a pattern for them to follow, and issued the fourth commandment, which confirmed the dignity even of slaves. For the second-generation Israelites, who were about to enter into the land of promise, obedience to the Sabbath command offered a foretaste of the rest they would enjoy once they took possession of the land (Deut. 3:20; 12:10; 25:19).

What does this mean for us today, since we aren't on the cusp of inheriting land promised by God? Working our fingers to the bone seven days a week degrades our dignity and makes us little better than slaves, no matter how big our bank account. The millionaire who works on weekends is in bondage just as much as the person who is barely getting by.

We aren't meant to be enslaved, to work twenty-four hours a day, seven days a week. It'll kill a person. Those compelled to give their lives to work experience higher levels of stress, depression, and anxiety. They're more prone to severe fatigue, surges of adrenaline (which can then increase cholesterol and decrease blood supply because of constricted capillaries and other blood vessels, potentially leading to heart disease), and thoughts of suicide.[7]

There needs to be a time once a week when we say, "You know what? That's enough! It's not that I've done everything I could do, but I've done everything I need to do for now." There is more to life than work. That's why God says we need to take a Sabbath, a day when we resist work and resist even thinking about work.

Last Friday evening, I was looking over my sermon for Sunday morning, trying to polish it a bit more. Then I thought, *I could spend an hour or two more on this message, but I've finally gotten to the point where it's good enough. It's not going to get much better than this, no matter how long I spend on it. I need to do something else.* We all need that in our lives—the time when we say, "Enough."

By the way, that time doesn't just have to come once a week. I want to suggest to you that it's good wisdom to have a finish line every day as well—a time when you say, "Once I've crossed this line, I'm finished." At a certain time in the evening, you say "Enough!" It doesn't mean that every dish has been washed, every piece of clothing is clean, and every phone call has been made, but it's enough for today, and you choose to rest.

God tells us to get off the gerbil wheel and rest because He has our well-being in mind, which is why He created a mini-vacation one day out of each week.

The Family

The Sabbath affirms the family. Inevitably, whenever we take a day off from work, we tend to spend it with family and friends, which gives us an opportunity to reconnect with our loved ones and repair the most important bonds in our lives. If you doubt this, ask the spouse of a workaholic whether it would enrich their marriage if their husband or wife took off at least one day a week.

The fact is, in today's technological world, there's emotional stress associated with work that sometimes is more taxing than the physical stress people endured a hundred years ago. You may have heard of William Wilberforce, a Christian who was a British member of Parliament in the early nineteenth century. Wilberforce was a man of great ambition. He led the effort to abolish the slave trade in Great Britain. He worked so tirelessly that his wife and friends feared he would ruin his already fragile health.

But on Sundays Wilberforce refused to work or even think about work. Instead, it was his time for rest and for worship. In one of his spiritual journals, Wilberforce wrote, "Blessed be God for this day of rest and religious occupation [Sunday], wherein earthly things assume their true size and comparative insignificance; ambition is stunted, and I hope my affections in some degree rise to things above."[8] I love that line "wherein earthly things assume their true size." Six days a week the things of this world are in our focus and can seem so large, but on the Sabbath, we turn away from our everyday concerns and see things as God sees them.

Unfortunately, a friend of Wilberforce's didn't come to the same conclusion. He abandoned his family by taking his own life. Thinking about his friend, who had given up on what Wilberforce called "Sunday consultations," Wilberforce wrote to a mutual friend, "If [their friend] had suffered his mind to enjoy such occasional remissions [from his toils], it is highly probable the strings would never have snapped as they did, from over-tension."[9]

Overexerting and overextending yourself isn't unhealthy only for your mental, emotional, and physical health but also for your family. Think about a rubber band. You can stretch a rubber band, but if you keep it stretched too long and too far, eventually it's going to snap. It's the same with us. There needs to come a time when we relax the tension. That day is the Sabbath.

Let me encourage you with a truth found in Exodus 31:17. God said, "For in six days the LORD made heaven and earth, but on the seventh day He ceased from labor, *and was refreshed*." Isn't that a neat thought? God was refreshed on the Sabbath. This tells me that on the Sabbath it's not enough just to quit working; we need to do something to refresh ourselves. This Sunday, go to church with your family or friends and think about how the singing and the sermon can refresh you. Then, do something with your loved ones that will recharge your batteries. Go out to lunch or a movie, or come home and watch a football game or take a nap.

I'm often asked about what I do on Sunday afternoons, after I'm through preaching. Amy and I grab lunch, sometimes with our grown children. But after that we go home, and I take off my suit and put on my pajamas. If I don't take a nap, I pop a bowl of popcorn, and Amy and I watch a movie. Then, depending on the time, I read before Amy and I have dinner. After dinner, I fix a bowl of Häagen-Dazs vanilla ice cream, and we watch another movie together. That's how I refresh myself—with family, starting with worshiping together.

Duty to God

The Sabbath affirms our duty to God. Every time you keep the Sabbath, you acknowledge your obligation to honor your Creator with your worship and praise. God made us as trichotomous beings: we are body, soul, and spirit. And there's no such thing as true refreshment that focuses only on the body and the emotions. For our refreshment to be complete, there has to be a spiritual component, and that's why we have Sundays. Sundays are a time for us to renew our relationship with God. Now, obviously during the week we ought to read our Bibles and pray. But there's something about setting aside a day or a portion of a day when we focus on our relationship with God and also on our relationship with other Christians.

I sometimes hear folks say they don't need to attend church on Sundays to have a healthy relationship with God. "All I need is Jesus and my Bible," they say. If you've ever said that, or know those who have, let me point out two passages related to this attitude. The first is Hebrews 10:24–25: "Let us consider how to stimulate one another to love and good deeds, not forsaking our own assembling together, as is the habit of some, but encouraging one another; and all the more as you see the day drawing near." Since we have a "great priest" in Christ, "over the house of God," the church (v. 21), it's our duty to Him to help those who struggle in their faith, who may not see or appreciate the purpose God has for them. We can only do that when we gather together as a community of faith within the church. Regular church attendance not only is a sign of obedience to the fourth commandment but also facilitates love for one another because it provides us with needed reminders and exhortations to persevere in the faith.

The second passage is Luke 4:16: "And [Jesus] came to Nazareth, where He had been brought up; and as was His custom, He entered the synagogue on the Sabbath, and stood up to read." If anyone could say they didn't need to attend church, it was Jesus. But He kept the law faithfully and fully, including the fourth commandment, going to the synagogue every Sabbath day, "as was His custom." Christ understood the best way to honor and worship God was in community with other believers. It's the same for us. We need a time when we come together collectively as believers and remember that we're part of something bigger than ourselves. There's something encouraging and edifying about Christians coming together and realizing they're not alone in the world.

Don't you just love being with other Christians on Sunday? I mean, for believers to be together, singing God's praises, hearing God's Word, seeing people we haven't seen all week—there's something invigorating about that. We need a time of community, and that time is the Sabbath when we come together.

By the way, the Sabbath not only benefits us spiritually, but when we fail to be at church on Sunday, we're depriving other Christians of something they desperately need. We in the body of Christ are connected to one another. And when you're not in your place on Sunday morning, it hurts the body of believers. When you're not in church on Sundays, that means there's one less voice singing the praises of God. There's one less person praying that somebody might come to know Christ. There's one less set of ears hearing the Word of God that transforms lives. When you're not in church on Sundays, there's one less person using his or her spiritual gifts to edify and build up other Christians. Your presence or lack of presence at church on Sundays really does make a difference. That's why God says we are to come together once a week. We're not to forsake our own assembling together.

If you say you need Jesus and want to follow Him, then follow His example. Observe the Sabbath commandment by attending church on Sunday.

God's Sovereignty

The Sabbath affirms God's sovereignty. In his commentary on Exodus, Warren Wiersbe wrote, "When the Jews observed the Sabbath, it was not only a mark of their devotion to the Lord, but it was also a witness to their pagan neighbors to whom the seventh day was just another day. By resting on the seventh day, the Jews were promoting their own welfare as well as that of their servants and farm animals, acknowledging the lordship of Jehovah over time and creation (Exod. 23:12)."[10]

Though it hardly seems like much of a witness, we, too, declare the same message of God's sovereignty over our lives whenever we obey the fourth commandment by ceasing from our work and celebrating our God in worship.

5

The Fifth Commandment: Honor Your Parents

Honor your father and your mother, that your days may be prolonged in the land which the LORD your God gives you.

Exodus 20:12

When my oldest daughter and her husband made me a grandfather, I was reminded of one of the greatest joys in life—placing children on your lap and reading them a story. Like any good grandfather, when my triplet grandchildren were born, I looked for stories that would build their character. In my search I found a book of German fairy tales collected by the Grimm brothers.

You're probably familiar with "Cinderella," "Little Red Riding Hood," and "Snow White and the Seven Dwarfs." But I bet you don't know the story "The Old Grandfather's Corner," in which a grandfather was made to sit in a corner. He was a feeble old man, and his hands shook. He lived with his son and daughter-in-law. At dinnertime, whenever he tried to eat his soup, more of it splashed on the tablecloth and floor than made it to his mouth. His daughter-in-law grew tired of washing the tablecloth and mopping the floor, so she consigned him to a corner, behind a screen, so the family wouldn't have to watch him. One day, his hands shook so badly that he dropped his bowl of soup, splattering it all over the floor and shattering the bowl. From that point on, his daughter-in-law served his meals in a wooden bowl.

Some days afterward, the father saw his young son fiddling with a couple of pieces of wood. He asked, "What are you making?" The boy said, "I am making a little bowl for papa and mama to eat their food in when I grow up."[1]

When you become a parent, you make your share of mistakes. When you become a grandparent, you get a sort of do-over. One of the things I learned as a father that I'm conscious of as a grandfather is that children imitate their parents and grandparents, just as the little boy in the fairy tale did. So, because I want my grandchildren to respect their parents and grandparents, I want to make sure my grandchildren see me demonstrate a deep and abiding respect for my own parents, even though they're already gone. In the words of Exodus 20:12, I want my grandchildren to honor their father and mother, which is the subject of this chapter.

However, before we get into the particulars, let's reorient ourselves. The first four commandments address our relationship with God—our vertical connection. The last six commandments address our relationships with others—our horizontal connections. This order is important. When asked about the most important commandment, Jesus said we are to love God *first* and love others *second* (Matt. 22:37–39). The point is simple: only when we're in a right relationship with God can we be in healthy relationships with one another.

When it comes to our relationships with others, God starts with our first and most important human relationship—the one we have with our father and mother. Just as we're to honor God because He has given us spiritual life, so we're to honor our parents because through them God gave us physical life.

As a pastor, I've seen over and over that how people relate to their parents affects how they relate in every other relationship in life, including their relationship with God. God understands the importance of the parent-child relationship. It's no accident that the very first commandment that deals with human relationships focuses on the parent-child relationship.

To get a firm grasp on the fifth commandment, we'll ask and answer four questions.

What's So Important about Families?

Obedience to the fifth commandment is particularly needed today since dishonor is so prevalent. Paul warned, "In the last days difficult times will come. For men will be lovers of self, lovers of money, boastful, arrogant, revilers, *disobedient to parents*, ungrateful, unholy" (2 Tim. 3:1–2)—and the list goes on, describing, in J. I. Packer's words, days of "decadence and apostasy."[2]

To shield us against this decadence and apostasy creeping into our families, here are five reasons that families are important.[3]

First, *the family is the basic structure of society*. That was true in ancient Israel, and it's true today. Martin Luther once said, "What is a city but a collection of houses where, if father and mother rule badly, and let children have their own way, then neither city nor town or village, district, kingdom, or empire, can be well and perfectly governed."[4] As the home goes, so goes the nation.

Second, *the parent-child relationship is the only lifelong relationship*. The relationship between parents and children lasts a lifetime. For this reason, it can be the trickiest relationship we ever manage, while at the same time one of the most joyful relationships we'll ever have. We enter this world in that relationship. We leave this world in that relationship, even if our parents precede us in death. As such, the fifth commandment directly addresses adult children of aging parents, not just children still living under their parents' roof. We could paraphrase the command like this: "Adult children, honor your aging father and mother, whose days have been long in the land, so that your days, too, might be long in the land."[5]

Third, *the parent-child relationship is the core of self-image*. How we think about ourselves is greatly impacted by our relationship with our father and mother. It's from our parents that we first learn, or fail to learn, the worth we have as human beings made in the image of God. Our parents' acceptance or rejection of us makes an indelible imprint on our souls, affecting our self-image and our future relationships.

Fourth, *the family is the incubator shaping attitudes toward authority*. Children who learn early on that there are boundaries in the home adjust better to the boundaries of the larger society. But children who have no boundaries in the home have a more difficult time adjusting to the boundaries of the larger society, whether at school, at work, or within the community governed by law. If children don't honor the people closest to them, then they won't honor people further removed from them. The best assurance that your children will respond to authority outside the home with wisdom, generosity, and grace is to make sure the authority at home is exercised with wisdom, generosity, and grace.

Fifth, *the family establishes a child's values*. Like the little boy in the Grimm fairy tale, children watch their parents and imitate them, picking up on what is valued and practiced in the home. If children see their parents acting disrespectfully, cutting corners, cheating, and lying, then those parents shouldn't be surprised when their children do the same. If the parents value money or education or recreation or athletics, the children soon pick up on that. If children see their parents saying "Thank you" and "Please," then they are more likely to value that as well.

When our girls were younger and Amy and I took them to a restaurant, they were always respectful to the waitstaff, saying "Thank you" and "Please," and "Yes, sir" and "Yes, ma'am." They sat respectfully and ate their meals. On occasion someone would comment on how well-behaved the girls were. Amy and I took it more as a compliment on our parenting than on the girls' nature because we worked hard to raise respectful, peaceful, and gracious children by demonstrating those same virtues with each other and people we encountered outside our home. Of course, when they occasionally misbehaved, we were not so quick to accept responsibility for that behavior!

It's also from parents that children learn the most important thing in life is serving God. By the way, it's no accident that the Hebrew word for "parents" is *horim*, which is related to the word for "teacher." Parents are and remain the first and foremost teachers children will ever have.

What Does It Mean to Honor?

The fifth commandment is the first and only time the word *honor* appears in the Ten Commandments. But the first four commandments in essence exhort us to honor God in thought, word, and deed because He is the Creator and Sovereign over all creation, including us, and because He is our "Father in heaven," as Jesus taught us to address Him. Therefore, He is worthy of our honor, or for His name to be hallowed (Matt. 6:9).

But that doesn't quite get to the heart of what it means to honor God or our parents. The Hebrew word translated as "honor" (*kabod*) has the same root as the word translated as "glory," which means to "make heavy or weighty." It's the idea of giving something substantial to a worthy individual. Heads of state do this when meeting for the first time, exchanging valuable gifts as a sign of respect. When used of God, we give Him glory and honor when we praise Him and make Him the center of our lives. In the same way, we honor our parents when we give them our obedience and respect, holding them in high esteem. To carry the title "mother" or "father" is a weighty responsibility. For that reason, as the Lord said in Leviticus 19:3, "Every one of you shall *reverence* his mother and his father."

Honor is the internal attitude we extend to those deserving of honor (Prov. 3:27; Rom. 13:7) through the outward actions of obedience, respect, reverence, love, and gratitude. As one expositor put it: "Obedience is the *duty*; honor is the disposition of which the obedience is born."[6]

Why Should We Honor Our Parents?

God's answer to this question could follow along the same lines of how we often answer our children when they ask why: "Because I said so." He could leave it at that—"I'm God and you're not. Do what I say." But I suspect the "Because I said so" answer doesn't sit any more comfortably with you than it does with your children. I've discovered three biblical reasons we should honor our parents. One is theological (concerning God), one is sociological (concerning the nation), and one is anthropological (concerning our elders).

The Theological Answer

Theologically, *attitudes toward parents mirror attitudes toward God.* It's interesting to think about Jesus's relationship with His earthly parents, Joseph and Mary. No one had a better attitude toward God than Jesus. After all, He was (and is) God incarnate—God in human flesh. And no one had a better attitude toward His parents and their authority over Him (even though He was and is God).

When Jesus was twelve years old, He and His family traveled from Nazareth to Jerusalem for the Passover. When it was time to go home, young Jesus disappeared. If you've ever lost a child in a crowd at the mall, the fair, or a ball game, you understand how frantic Mary and Joseph were when they couldn't find their boy. They searched throughout the city for *three days*, finally finding Him in the temple courtyards talking with the elders of Israel.

Mary said to Him, "Son, why have You treated us this way? Behold, Your father and I have been anxiously looking for You" (Luke 2:48).

The first part of Jesus's answer sounds like something any twelve-year-old might say: "Why is it that you were looking for Me?" A cursory reading makes it sound like Jesus was being disrespectful. He wasn't. He esteemed His earthly parents, but He reminded them—in the second part of His answer—that He had come on a mission: "Did you not know that I had to be in My Father's house?" (v. 49).

Granted, Mary and Joseph didn't fully understand that answer, but they in no way took it as snarky or demeaning. Nevertheless, they insisted Jesus go with them that very minute. And here's the wonderful part: He did. "He went down with them and came to Nazareth, and He continued in subjection to them" (v. 51). Can you imagine? The perfect Son of God subjected Himself to imperfect parents. It's mind-blowing! But Jesus did. His obedience—the honor He showed Joseph and Mary—resulted in His mental, physical, spiritual, and social well-being (v. 52).

The Sociological Answer

Sociologically, *anarchy in the home leads to anarchy in the nation.* I hinted at this truth earlier, but let's look at it a bit more closely. There are two aspects to this: one involving the promise found in Exodus 20:12 and the other involving the principle demonstrated in the nation of Israel.

First, let's look at *the promise of the fifth commandment.* In Ephesians 6:2, Paul said this commandment was "the first commandment with a promise."[7] What was that promise? It's found in Exodus 20:12 (and Deut. 5:16): "that your days may be prolonged in the land which the LORD your God gives you." This isn't a guarantee of *long life* enjoyed in the promised land. Rather, it's an assurance of *abundant life* enjoyed in the promised land. It's something akin to Jesus's statement of purpose: "I came that they may have life, and have it abundantly" (John 10:10). Though the promise could be seen as a personal blessing to every individual who obeys the command, it clearly had national implications for Israel—namely, that if they were known as a people who honored their elders (parents in particular), then they would permanently possess the land under God's rule and become a blessing to their neighbors.

This goes back to the covenant God made with Abraham in Genesis 12, when the Lord vowed to make Abraham a great nation in possession of the land God had promised to him (vv. 1–2). The purpose of this covenant was that the nation coming from Abraham's family "shall be a blessing" (v. 2). God made it even plainer in verse 3: "In you all the families of the earth will be blessed." Ultimately, this covenant of national blessing was fulfilled in the birth, life, death, and resurrection of Jesus Christ, the descendant of Abraham. Everyone who has placed faith in Jesus has received the blessing promised to and through Abraham. We've been set free from sin and death and given a new life to be enjoyed both in the here and now and in the eternal future to come. We've been placed into a new family—the family of God, the church—and have been given the indwelling presence of the Holy Spirit, who guides us, protects us, and intercedes for us. These and other blessings belong to everyone who believes in the name of the Lord Jesus Christ, who is the Son of God and the descendant of Abraham, through whom the blessing was pledged and given.

However, what Christians *aren't* promised is a particular piece of land. In Ephesians 6:1, Paul interpreted the first word of the fifth commandment ("Honor") as "obey," and he interpreted the promise of abundant life for Christians this way: "so that it may be well with you, and that you may live long on the earth" (v. 3). The principle is the same today. Children who honor godly parents through obedience avoid perils that might otherwise shorten their lives and that plague our nation: drug and alcohol abuse, crimes against property and persons, and suicide.

Second, let's look at *the principle of the fifth commandment.* I once heard a pastor who preached on Exodus 20:12 say, "Those who foster a society where old age is honored will reap the benefits of that society as they grow old." The simple truth is, God blesses a society that honors the family.

It's not coincidental that, in an effort to exert control over people, totalitarian regimes attack the family, especially the importance of fathers in the lives of children. Tyrants seek to transfer allegiance from the family to the state. A professor at a prestigious university not too many years ago did a promotional video for the cable news company MSNBC in which she said, "We have to break through our kind of private idea that kids belong to their parents or kids belong to their family and recognize that kids belong to whole communities."[8] In other words, children belong to the state. As the power of one increases, the power of the other decreases.

When the nation of Judah fell to the Babylonian tyrant Nebuchadnezzar, a distinguishing mark of national evil was the disrespect shown to elders. Jeremiah wrote of this in Lamentations: "Elders were not respected" (5:12). Instead, they were run off "from the gate," where the people use to come for counsel (v. 14).

The Anthropological Answer

Anthropologically, *appreciating elders maintains their dignity in an undignified world.* While the fifth commandment specifically concerns the parent-child relationship, it can be extended as a command to treat all elders with deference, just as Paul exhorted in 1 Timothy 5:1–2 and Peter instructed in 1 Peter 5:5. But such respect begins at home since our parents are the first and most important elders in our lives.

There's little doubt we live in a youth-oriented culture, where, in the words of one grayheaded theologian, "Young people . . . are more prone than ever to write off their parents as clueless old fuddy-duddies."[9] Not just their parents but anyone older than themselves. When the young despise the dignity of old age, they not only show themselves as undignified but also despise the Lord in the process. How can I say that? Well, buried in the Old Testament book of Leviticus is this forgotten gem of advice, where the Lord linked reverence for the elderly with reverence for Him: "You shall rise up before the grayheaded and honor the aged, and you shall revere your God; I am the LORD" (19:32).

Whenever I encounter seminary students, I always tell them to take as many classes from the gray heads as they can. Not only are older professors experts in their subject matter but they have lived experience that can't be learned from a book. I remind these students, "The glory of young men is their strength, and the honor of old men is their gray hair"—wisdom born of pain (Prov. 20:29).

How Do We Honor Our Parents?

Warren Wiersbe warned, "The elderly are the only outcast group that everybody expects to join because nobody wants the alternative. But how we treat them today will help to determine how we're treated tomorrow, because we reap what we sow."[10] Sowing a spirit of honor for our parents is a lifelong pursuit. I've identified four ways, based on four stages of life, we are to do that in obedience to the fifth commandment.

Obedience

As children, we honor our parents by obeying them. In Colossians 3:20, Paul instructed children to obey their parents "in all things." But in Ephesians 6:1, he qualified that statement with the words "in the Lord." Here's what Paul meant: children are to obey their parents as long as their parents' instructions don't contradict the teaching of the Lord.[11] For example, if a parent tells his or her child to lie on college applications to get into a better school, then that child isn't obligated to obey. The principle of Acts 5:29 applies: "We must obey God rather than men" because a child's primary responsibility is to the Lord, then to parents.

Children are only required to obey their parents while they're still living under their parents' authority. When a child becomes an adult, he or she is no longer required to obey parental authority—though the child is still duty-bound to honor his or her parents. The exception to this is when adult children are living under their parents' roof. A colleague of mine has a son who's working on an online master's degree. To save on expenses, his son is living at home and working part-time. Though the son is an adult, he is still required to do chores around the house: mow the lawn, wash the dishes, and take out the trash. He honors his parents by obeying them in doing these things, thereby pleasing the Lord (Col. 3:20).

Respect

As young adults, we honor our parents by respecting them. One of the best ways to show respect for parents is to seek their counsel and give serious attention to their advice. Proverbs is filled with counsel and advice from a wise father to his son. For example, Solomon wrote, "My son, obey your father's commands, and don't neglect your mother's instruction. Keep their words always in your heart. Tie them around your neck. When you walk, their counsel will lead you. When you sleep, they will protect you. When you wake up, they will advise you. For their command is a lamp and their instruction a light; their corrective discipline is the way to life" (Prov. 6:20–23 NLT).

Whether it has to do with choosing a spouse or choosing a career, listening to the counsel of your parents is not only wise but a way to honor them.

Of course, that doesn't mean you have to follow their counsel blindly. I speak from experience when I say that parents aren't perfect. We don't always get it right. There are times when I've given my daughters career advice that in retrospect was based more on my gifts and interests than their unique gifts and interests. Fortunately, they've learned how to accept the good and reject the not-so-good counsel I sometimes offer.

As we become adults, God has a plan for us to move from dependence to independence from our parents. We see this plan in Genesis 2:24. Moses wrote, "For this reason a man shall leave his father and his mother, and be joined to his wife; and they shall become one flesh." This leaving that a man or a woman does isn't just a physical leaving; it's an emotional leaving. There comes a time when you emotionally leave your father and mother in order to cleave to the spouse God has ordained for you. And it's very important that this emotional leaving take place if a home is to have any chance of surviving.

I remember a few years ago a woman came to me. She and her husband had been visiting our church, and they liked being in a church where the Bible was taught, but the wife had a problem. She said, "Pastor, my husband and I both want to join this church, but if I do it, my mother is going to be upset. I grew up in a different denomination. My mother, my grandmother, my great-grandmother—they were all members of that denomination, and she's going to be disappointed if I join this church." I explained to her that she needed to leave her mother emotionally, and if the Lord was leading, she and her husband should join our church. In marriage, our relationship to our parents changes. No longer are they authority figures in our lives. Nevertheless, we ought to seek their advice. It doesn't mean we have to follow our parents' advice all the time, but we would be wise to seek it.

As young adults, our duty isn't to obey our parents but to respect them. All throughout our lives we ought to consider that godly counsel we may have received from our parents.

Support

As middle-aged adults, we honor our parents by supporting them. Many of us are in the "sandwich generation"—that time of life when we have children at home, usually teenagers or young adults, and aging parents who need assistance. Our children are at the stage of moving from dependence to independence, but our parents are at the stage of moving from independence to dependence.

In a practical sense, honoring our parents by supporting them means assisting them financially if necessary. In Mark 7,

Jesus had a run-in with the Pharisees (the Jewish religious leaders of His day) about the fifth commandment. Jesus said, "You are experts at setting aside the commandment of God in order to keep your tradition" (v. 9). He reminded them of the fifth commandment and then added this from Leviticus 20:9: "He who speaks evil of father or mother is to be put to death" (Mark 7:10).[12] Jesus clarified that the Pharisees were violating God's command by quoting one of their teachings that allowed them to wiggle out of supporting their parents financially: "If a man says to his father or his mother, whatever I have that would help you is Corban (that is to say, given to God), you no longer permit him to do anything for his father or his mother" (vv. 11–12). *Corban* was the idea that you could dedicate to God a certain amount of money you hadn't actually given yet. You still possessed the money and could use it, but the tradition barred you from giving it to others, even to needy parents. That's why Jesus said, "Thus [you invalidate] the word of God by your tradition which you have handed down" (v. 13).

The Pharisees had gotten to the point that honoring their man-made traditions was more important than honoring God's Word—and in the process they dishonored their parents because they valued their money more than they valued their parents. But the principle Jesus established is clear: when it comes to your obligation to financially support your parents and your obligation to financially support God's ministry, your greater responsibility is to provide for your parents.

Let me add that supporting your parents in their waning years isn't just financial; it's also emotional and spiritual. Make sure you're calling your parents and speaking with them on a regular basis. Take them out to lunch or dinner occasionally—on your dime. Go with them to their doctors' appointments and run errands for them. Bring them to church with you. Do whatever is needed for their well-being.

Reverence

As adults who've lost parents, we honor our parents by reverencing them. I didn't live through the sandwich years with my parents because they died fairly early in life. But I try to honor them by the way I speak about them to my children, grandchildren, other family members, and friends. I remember shortly after my father passed away, I was under a deadline to finish a book. I had used an illustration of him in one chapter, but when I read the proofs, it dawned on me that a reader could get the wrong impression about my father. I hadn't written anything negative, but the way I worded the illustration could lead someone to the wrong assumption about him. So I reworked the illustration to make sure no one could reach a conclusion that my father was anything but an honorable and godly man.

You also honor or dishonor your departed parents by your memory of them. Most of us have at least one memory we cherish about our parents, even if we have more than one we'd like to forget. Regardless of whether we had good or bad parents, we're all obligated to obey the fifth commandment—even though our parents may be gone. How can you do that? It's impossible to forget bad memories. And I'd never tell you to sweep them under the proverbial rug, pretending they never happened. However, you can ask God to help you forgive your parents. Be honest with the Lord, saying something like, "God, my mom/my dad really hurt me as a child. But I choose to honor them by forgiving them, just as I want You to forgive me." Name the hurts and let God work so you can release those hurts into His forgiving care. Then choose to focus on the good things you remember about your parents, thanking God for those things. Paul wrote, "Whatever is true, whatever is honorable, whatever is right, whatever is pure, whatever is lovely, whatever is of good repute . . . dwell on these things" (Phil. 4:8).

Here's one last way you can honor your deceased parents: live in such a way that would please them—that upholds the family name. There's something healthy about living your life according to the highest ideals established by your parents.

Like many of you, I have parents who are already gone, and I miss them. But I'm grateful there was no unfinished business left between us when they passed away. They knew how much I loved and respected them. There was closure to that relationship. And I'll be eternally grateful for that.

One day, if it hasn't already happened, you're going to get a telephone call telling you that your last parent is gone. I pray when that day comes, there'll be no unfinished business between you and them. How can you make sure that happens? By obeying the fifth commandment and honoring your father and mother.

6

The Sixth Commandment:
Preserve Life

You shall not murder.

Exodus 20:13

A key indicator of the health of a society is whether that society is just or unjust. And a key indicator of a society's level of justice is whether that society values human life.

Not long ago, I caught the movie adaptation of Cormac McCarthy's Pulitzer Prize–winning novel *The Road*. It's the story about a father and son trying to survive in a postapocalyptic world. It's a world that's dying, and with it, its humanity. Animals, birds, and fish are all but extinct. Groups of people roam the streets and woods like packs of dogs, looking for food. Their main diet is the meat of men—they're cannibals.

In the nuclear fallout, the boy has never seen blue skies or green grass or autumn leaves. Nor has he known what it's like to live in peace, to trust another human being other than his father. The father struggles to keep the hope of humanity alive for himself and his son. At one point, the father tells the boy, "You have to carry the fire"—his way of saying the boy not only needs to live but to live nobly.[1] In the midst of a world filled with humans who no longer value human lives but for the meals they provide, the father tells his boy to live in such a way that his life and the lives of others are kept precious.

Watching *The Road* reminded me of another story—a true one. It took place within a broken society where "every intent of the thoughts of [mankind's] heart was only evil continually" (Gen. 6:5). God was "sorry" He had created human beings and was "grieved" by their sin (v. 6). He decided to "blot out" every man, woman, and child, along with the rest of creation (v. 7), with one caveat: Noah and his family would survive. They carried the fire and "found favor in the eyes of the LORD" because "Noah walked with God" (vv. 8–9).

You know the story. Noah built an ark to save his family, along with a male and female pair of every animal the Lord chose, from the coming deluge that would flood the earth. What you may not know is the reason God decided to destroy the earth. Yes, there was immorality and corruption, but God focused on the fact that "the earth was filled with violence" (v. 11). The people of Noah's day, just like the people in McCarthy's novel, had no regard for human life.

After the flood subsided and Noah and his family emerged from the ark, God made a covenant with Noah never to destroy the earth again by flood (9:11). The Lord also instructed Noah, "Whoever sheds man's blood, by man his blood shall be shed, for in the image of God He made man" (v. 6). Later, this covenant was incorporated into the covenant the Lord made with the nation of Israel, which was governed by a set of laws. One in particular dealt with the value of human life—the sixth commandment: "You shall not murder" (Exod. 20:13).

In the original Hebrew, commandments six through eight are conveyed as two-word imperatives: "No murder." "No adultery." "No theft." Each concerns how we value other human beings: their lives, their marriages, and their possessions. We'll look at each in turn, but for now let's look at the command to preserve life by answering three questions and applying one challenge.

What Does the Sixth Commandment Say?

The translation of Exodus 20:13 in the King James Version of the Bible says, "Thou shalt not kill." In Hebrew, it's simply *Lo ratsach*. However, the translation "kill" fails to capture the precise meaning of the Hebrew word *ratsach*. Within the larger context of Hebrew literature, *ratsach* doesn't mean "kill" per se. That wouldn't make sense, as God doesn't forbid all *killing*. He made allowances for capital punishment, even before the Mosaic law was given to Israel (Gen. 9:6),[2] as well as just warfare (Deut. 20:10–18). These two forms of killing are, at least in theory, sanctioned under law and controlled by the state.

The Lord also made a provision for killing in self-defense, if taking the life of an intruder was the only means of protecting your life or the lives of your family (Exod. 22:2). In the Old Testament, this ordinance was restricted to nighttime because during the light of day a person would have greater opportunity to call for help and identify the intruder (v. 3). However, I believe that anytime an intruder is brandishing and threatening to use a weapon and your necessary actions of self-defense result in his or her death, whether at night or during the day, you haven't violated the sixth commandment.

Whatever your personal opinions on capital punishment, warfare, and self-defense, it's clear that each of these activities involves (or potentially involves) the killing of a human being. Therefore, the sixth commandment doesn't refer to state-sanctioned killing (capital punishment and just warfare) or killing as a result of self-defense. So what is included under the sixth commandment?

Based on how *ratsach* is used in other Hebrew passages, I believe the sixth commandment prohibits premeditated killing—murder.[3] The New American Standard Bible (and other modern versions) is correct in translating Exodus 20:13 this way: "You shall not *murder*."

What Does the Sixth Commandment Cover?

The sixth commandment prohibits the taking of a human life without divine authorization. All life belongs to God. He is the Giver of life, and He is the only one who has the right to take life—or to make legal and moral provisions for the taking of life. The murderer, then, commits an extreme act of arrogance since he or she, a mere creature, assumes the position of the Creator God, co-opting a right that belongs to Him alone.

That's clear enough. But obviously there are other ways in which someone might take the life of another person short of premeditated murder, such as involuntary manslaughter or death through neglect. Does the sixth commandment encompass these? I don't think so because the punishment for violating the sixth commandment is death, as we'll see when we address the next question.

We certainly are to do everything in our power to prevent accidental death. In Deuteronomy 22:8, the Lord said to the people, "When you build a new house, you shall make a parapet for your roof, so that you will not bring bloodguilt on your house if anyone falls from it." In ancient Israel the roof became another room, one to sleep on during hot nights or to enjoy under a canopy during the day where you might pick up a breeze off the Mediterranean Sea. If you didn't construct a parapet—a low wall—around the roofline and someone fell to their death, you would be guilty of neglect. Adding a parapet, just like we build fences around backyard swimming pools, was a way of loving your neighbors and preserving their lives. However, failure to do so isn't in view in the sixth commandment, any more than if a child tragically drowns in a pool that isn't properly fenced. As we'll discuss in more detail later in this chapter, the Old Testament clearly differentiated between accidental killing and premeditated killing.

There are specific forms of killing—or devaluing human life—that are covered in the sixth commandment. I've divided them into acts of murder, attitudes that lead to murder, and activities short of murder.

Acts of Murder

I want to be sensitive here, but we need to call things what they really are. So if you know anyone who's been a victim of one of these acts, or if you've considered committing one of these acts, please seek pastoral and professional help.

Homicide. From the first murder, committed by the son of Adam and Eve, until today, the inhumanity shown to our fellow human beings by taking their lives out of anger, greed, spite, or revenge proves we live in a sin-sickened world. In the book of Hosea, the Lord said to the people, "The Lord has a case against the inhabitants of the land, because there is no faithfulness or kindness or knowledge of God in the land. There is swearing, deception, murder, stealing and adultery. They employ violence, so that bloodshed follows bloodshed. Therefore the land mourns, and everyone who lives in it languishes" (4:1–3). This could be said of any country in the world today, including the United States.

Suicide. Some of the saddest experiences I have had as a pastor are presiding over funeral services for those who have taken their lives. I always tell family members that suicide isn't an unpardonable sin and assure them that if their loved one was a Christian, he or she is in heaven. Many times those who take their lives do so out of desperation, believing Satan's lie that there is no hope for them. If you know of someone who is talking about suicide frequently, you need to encourage them to talk to a Christian counselor and/or Christian psychiatrist as soon as possible.

But our compassion for those who take their lives—and those who are left behind—shouldn't prevent us from saying clearly that suicide is akin to murder because it's the premeditated, volitional killing of self. Julie Gossack, who suffered through the suicides of five family members, wrote, "Suicide is not a genetic trait nor is it a family curse. Suicide is a sinful choice made by an individual. This statement is neither unloving nor disrespectful. It is the truth. I dearly loved my family members that committed suicide, but their choices were sinful and not righteous."[4]

Euthanasia. Euthanasia is sometimes referred to as assisted suicide. As of this writing, nine states and the District of Columbia have euthanasia laws on the books.[5] They're fraught with moral and ethical questions. The most pressing is whether these laws allow for the killing of so-called undesirables—the aged and infirm who become a burden on hospitals and insurance companies. That's what's happening in the Netherlands, where decisions are being made about whether the lives of the elderly or the terminally ill are worth saving. Physician-assisted suicide is not like the termination of a treatment, like a cancer patient refusing additional chemotherapy or radiation to regain some quality of life; it is, in fact, the termination of a life.

There's nothing compassionate about taking human life, no matter the method. But there's everything compassionate about giving consideration to the helpless (Ps. 41:1).

Abortion. People ask me, "Where does the Bible speak about abortion?" Certainly we see this issue addressed in Psalm 139, which says we are knit together in our mother's womb and that all of our days are in God's book before there is yet one of them. But here's another passage. Across the page from the Ten Commandments is a law governing injury to a baby while still in the mother's womb. It reads in part, "If men struggle with each other and strike a woman with child ... [and] there is ... injury [to the child], then you shall appoint as a penalty life for life" (Exod. 21:22–23). Writing on this passage, theologian John Calvin said, "The fetus, though enclosed in the womb of its mother, is already a human being, and it is almost a monstrous crime to rob it of the life which it has not yet begun to enjoy."[6]

Though many in our world disagree, the abortion of a child created in the image of God is nothing short of murder.

Attitudes That Lead to Murder

In my book *18 Minutes with Jesus*, I addressed the motivations behind murder, so I won't spend a lot of time on that here.[7] Suffice it to say, in general, the Pharisees taught that the sixth commandment prohibited literal homicide. Jesus taught that the commandment also covered the attitudes behind homicide (Matt. 5:21–22). As John Calvin wrote, "This commandment . . . prohibits the murder of the heart, and requires a sincere desire to preserve our brother's life. The hand, indeed, commits the murder, but the mind, under the influence of wrath and hatred, conceives it."[8]

There was no excuse for the Pharisees to misinterpret the sixth commandment, but they did. Jesus revealed their true motive behind their strict interpretation of God's command: they wanted to appear righteous before the people by not committing the *act* of murder, while still exhibiting *attitudes* that sometimes lead to murder. Jesus identified three such attitudes. Let's look at them quickly.

Anger. Jesus said, "I say to you that everyone who is angry with his brother shall be guilty before the court" (v. 22). The kind of anger Jesus was referring to here is an attitude that broods over revenge. The classic story of Ahab and the White Whale in Herman Melville's *Moby-Dick* is a good illustration of this type of anger. The whale had taken Ahab's leg, and Ahab was consumed with a bitterness that boiled over into vengeance. However, in the end, his bitterness consumed not only himself but also all his crew save one.

Insults. Jesus went on to say, "Whoever says to his brother, 'You good-for-nothing,' shall be guilty before the supreme court" (v. 22). The Aramaic word translated as "good-for-nothing" is *raca*, which refers to someone's mental aptitude. It means "empty-headed." It's obviously meant as an insult, like calling someone a *dimwit*, an *airhead*, a *dingbat*, an *imbecile*, or an *idiot*. It sounds childish and harmless, but it's not.

Children and teenagers are particularly adept at insulting others. When my daughters were growing up, I told them in no uncertain terms that they should never use the S-word—*stupid*—when talking about someone. I let them know, as far as I was concerned, that this S-word was a curse word directed at an image bearer of God, calling into question that image bearer's intelligence.

Defamation. Lastly, Jesus said, "Whoever says, 'You fool,' shall be guilty enough to go into the fiery hell" (v. 22). The Greek word translated as "fool" is *moros*, from where we get our word *moron*. It's meant to denigrate someone's moral character—to tarnish their reputation. It's slander or character assassination. Solomon wrote, "A good name is to be more desired than great wealth" (Prov. 22:1). And he also wrote, "With his mouth the godless man destroys his neighbor" (11:9). Calling someone a "fool" defames that person, murdering his or her good name.

Taken together, these three attitudes work in a sort of wicked harmony that looks something like this: First, I'm angry with you, whether justified or not. Second, if I don't deal with my anger appropriately I'll question your worth as a human being, insulting your intelligence—"You're stupid"—and then insulting your character—"You're disgusting." Finally, I'll hold you in contempt—"I wish you were dead"—which is just another way of saying, "You're not worthy of being called a human being." At this stage, I couldn't care less whether you're hurt or not. In fact, I'll give no consideration to you at all—you're dead to me. But if I did, it would result in murderous thoughts.

Just as *acts* of murder rob someone of their life, *attitudes* of murder rob them of their humanity, their personhood, and their dignity as image bearers. The apostle John wrote, "Anyone who hates a brother or sister is a murderer, and you know that no murderer has eternal life residing in him" (1 John 3:15 NIV).

Whenever you verbally assault somebody out of anger, out of bitterness, you're destroying something of value. You're verbally assaulting God's creation, which is analogous to murder, Jesus said. And by the way, just because someone is not a Christian gives us no right to assault them verbally. No matter how unrighteous someone may be, he or she is still a human being God created.

Activities Short of Murder

Besides the acts and attitudes of murder, the sixth commandment also covers *cruelty* and general *violence*. When Cain asked, "Am I my brother's keeper?" (Gen. 4:9), little did he know the answer to that question was a resounding yes. There may come times when we have to "go and do the same" as the good Samaritan (Luke 10:37) and protect our neighbor's life or well-being (vv. 30–36).[9]

Recently, I saw a video of a good Samaritan by the name of David Eubank, a former US Army Special Forces Ranger. He has a relief organization that goes into combat zones to offer medical aid and other assistance to civilians caught in the middle of warfare. The video I watched was filmed in Mosul, Iraq, in 2017. Eubank and a couple of US Special Forces members were standing behind a tank under heavy fire. Across a rock-strewn field were civilians cowering next to a bombed-out building. On his command, the two Special Forces members jumped from behind the tank and began firing while Eubank dashed across the field and gathered up a little girl in his arms, and then ran back, saving her life. Summing up what it means to be a good neighbor and to uphold the sixth commandment by protecting the lives of others, Eubank quoted John 15:13: "Greater love has no one than this, that one lay down his life for his friends."[10]

By the way, while we're talking about activities that lead to murder, let me make a secondary application here: God is utterly opposed to violence. When we read through the Old Testament law, we find prohibition after prohibition against physically striking another person. Why is that? Because human beings are objects of value to God. God is the one who creates life, He values life, and therefore He hates any kind of violence.

People ask me, "Pastor, what do you say to a woman who is living in an abusive marriage where her husband is subjecting her and her children to violence?" There is this screwed-up thinking out there that says a woman is supposed to stay in that situation. That's absurd, and that's a violation of the Word of God! Human life is valuable to God. And God hates violence.

Why Is the Punishment for Violating the Sixth Commandment So Severe?

In Matthew 5:22, Jesus upped the ante on the punishment for those who violate the spirit of the sixth commandment. *Anger* results in a guilty charge before "the court," the local magistrate. *Insults* lead to a guilty charge before "the supreme court," the Sanhedrin (the Jewish judicial body of Jesus's day). And *defamation* results in being tossed behind the fiery bars of hell. Jesus was speaking in hyperbole, meaning those who exhibit such attitudes are *worthy* of being found guilty on the charges of murder in a court of law because they wished someone dead or demeaned someone's mental ability or assassinated someone's character.

But when it came to the outright act of murder, there was no wiggle room on whether someone ought to go to court and, if found guilty, be punished. In Israel, murder was a capital offense. The Lord said, "He who strikes a man so that he dies shall surely be put to death. . . . If . . . a man acts presumptuously toward his neighbor, so as to kill him craftily, you are to take him even from My altar, that he may die" (Exod. 21:12, 14).[11]

However, as I mentioned earlier, accidental killings *weren't* capital offenses.[12] In Deuteronomy 19, the Lord offered a plausible what-if scenario. What if a man "kills his friend unintentionally, not hating him previously—as when a man goes into the forest with his friend to cut wood, and his hand swings the axe to cut down the tree, and the iron head slips off the handle and strikes his friend so that he dies" (vv. 4–5)? What happens to "the manslayer" (v. 4)?

Well, "he may flee to one of [the] cities" set aside to protect him (v. 5). Earlier, God said, "I will appoint you a place to which he may flee" (Exod. 21:13). Those places, six of them, were known as "cities of refuge" (Deut. 19:1–13). If a person accidentally killed someone, this manslayer could flee to a city of refuge to be protected from family members seeking revenge and live there until the case was adjudicated. If the death was ruled manslaughter, the one who committed the crime had to forfeit his liberty and not leave the city of refuge until the death of the high priest. At that time, having paid for his crime, he could return to his hometown without fear from "the blood avenger" (Num. 35:6–28).

Right about now you may be thinking, *That's fascinating, but it doesn't answer the question why violating the sixth command-ment carried such a heavy penalty.* Fair enough. The answer is simple: because human life is valuable—it is a gift from God, and we bear His image. If God didn't prescribe capital punish-ment for murder, He would devalue the life of the victim and could no longer call Himself the Lord of justice. Likewise, if a society doesn't prescribe capital punishment for murder, it devalues the life of the victim and can no longer call itself just.

God is the Creator of human life, breathing into every man, woman, and child the breath of life, thereby creating us in His image (Gen. 1:26–27; 2:7). David expanded on the precious-ness of human life in Psalm 139:13–16 when he described in intricate detail how God fashioned human beings. Then in verses 17–18, he wrote, "How precious are your thoughts about me, O God. They cannot be numbered! I can't even count them; they outnumber the grains of sand! And when I wake up, you are still with me!" (NLT).

Is it any wonder the Lord was outraged when Cain mur-dered his brother Abel (Gen. 4:8)? God asked Cain, "Where is Abel your brother?" (v. 9). God knew where Abel was, so this question was an opportunity for Cain to come clean. But he didn't. Instead, he doubled down on his crime (v. 9). Seeth-ing anger may lead to murder, as was the case with Cain, but murder never cools the anger. At its heart, Cain's anger wasn't directed at Abel; it was directed at God. Cain became embittered because Abel's sacrifice found favor with the Lord and his didn't (vv. 4–5). But Cain couldn't strike down God, so he targeted the next best thing: one of God's image bearers, his brother Abel.

However, God in His grace gave Cain another opportunity to confess his crime. "What have you done?" the Lord asked (v. 10). This time Cain remained silent, so God said it straight: "The voice of your brother's blood is crying to Me from the ground" for justice (v. 10).

Up until this point no one had ever seen a dead human body, much less a murdered one. Can you image Adam and Eve finding the lifeless body of their son Abel in the field? Perhaps nobody understood the value of human life more than Adam and Eve. They themselves were alive because God had breathed the breath of life into them. They realized that life was a gift from God, and no one had the right to take what God had given. They lost two sons that day—one to death, the other as an outcast (vv. 11–14, 16). Only the grace of God stayed His hand from killing Cain.

How You Can Keep the Sixth Commandment

In a scene in Larry McMurtry's novel *Lonesome Dove*, a hardened murderer by the name of Blue Duck wants to gamble with a gang of cutthroats. When one of them refuses, Blue Duck shoots him without warning. One man says, "By God, life's cheap up here on the . . . Canadian [River]." Blue Duck responds, "Cheap, and it might get cheaper."[13]

We're living in a world where human life is cheap. And while we have little power to do anything to make the world see the value of life, we have power enough in our individual lives to value those made in the image of God—to preserve life and "carry the fire." Here's how:

If you're in an abusive situation, for the sake of yourself and that of your children (if you have them), get out as soon as possible and find help.

If you struggle with thoughts of suicide, or you've attempted to take your life, seek help immediately. Speak with a close and trusted friend, a pastor, or a counselor. If you have nowhere else to turn, call the National Suicide Prevention Lifeline: (800) 273-8255 or 988.

If you're able, give your time and treasure to shelters that care for abused women and mothers, or pro-life organizations that provide help not only for the baby in the womb but also for the mother who carries the baby and the father who conceived the baby. Being pro-life is more than just picketing abortion clinics; it's supporting families after the baby has been born.

If you're able, volunteer or give money to support relief organizations that provide medical services, bring healthy food and clean water, construct homes, and provide other services to those in need.

If you have elderly neighbors, make sure they're cared for—that they have food, their lawn is mowed, repairs to their house are attended to, and anything else that is necessary for their well-being.

If you are bitter at a parent for mistreatment, a spouse for unfaithfulness, or a friend for betrayal, then root out that bitterness. Ask God to do some gardening in your heart—to prune you and make you more like Christ. I can tell you, there's nothing more Christlike than a wronged Christian who forgives the wrong.

You can think of other practical ways to demonstrate the value of human life.

One last note—John Calvin wrote, "Scripture notes a two-fold equity on which [the sixth] commandment is founded. Man is both the image of God and our flesh. Wherefore, if we would not violate the image of God, we must hold the person of man sacred—if we would not divest ourselves of humanity, we must cherish our own flesh."[14]

In short, we must "carry the fire."

7

The Seventh Commandment: Keep Marriage Holy

You shall not commit adultery.

Exodus 20:14

Only a fool says sinning isn't pleasant—at least initially. And sexual sin may be the most pleasant of all—initially. Solomon knew that. He's the one who wrote, "Stolen water is sweet; and bread eaten in secret is pleasant" (Prov. 9:17). But after a while, what was sweet sours and what was delicious decays, leading to death (v. 18).

Don't believe me? Let me tell you the tale of two families: husbands and wives married a long time, three children each, and each active in their local church. The husband in each family engaged in an ongoing and undetected adulterous affair. But in time—as Scripture says, "Be sure your sin will find you out" (Num. 32:23)—the illicit relationship of each was discovered. One husband confessed his sin and asked his wife and kids for forgiveness. He broke off the adulterous relationship and submitted to counseling.

However, the other husband made excuses for his sin. And though he asked his wife for forgiveness, he was unwilling to attend counseling and struggled with breaking his adulterous relationship. In the end, the one man saved his marriage and the couple has celebrated over sixty years together. The other man destroyed his marriage and nearly destroyed his family.

Adultery is the reigning sin of our times. Even as far back as seven hundred and fifty years before the birth of Christ, adultery was part of human existence. At that time, God directed one of His prophets, Hosea, to marry a professional adulteress—a prostitute. Can you imagine getting that message from the Lord? God said to Hosea, in essence, "Go to the street corner and pick out a prostitute as your bride." What must his father and mother have said when he brought her home? "Mom and Dad, I'd like you to meet Gomer; she's a streetwalker." Yet that's what God told Hosea to do (1:2). It was through Hosea's troubled marriage with Gomer, and her unfaithfulness to him, that the Lord challenged His unfaithful people, whom He called "adulterers," to return to Him (7:4).

We can go even further back than Hosea and Gomer and find adultery. Seven hundred years before Hosea, the Lord laid down an unequivocal command we know as the seventh commandment: "You shall not commit adultery" (Exod. 20:14). It's the sad tale we'll tell in this chapter.

God Is Pro-Sex but Anti-Adultery

It's tricky business writing about sex since men and women, marrieds and singles, the divorced and the abused have so many different perspectives, hang-ups, and scares. I'd never be able to address every question or concern you might have, but I want you to understand this clearly: God is pro-sex.[1] He absolutely loves sex.

Think about it. Who invented the idea of sex? Where did it come from? I mean, can't you just picture God in heaven one day thinking, *I've got a great idea for what would be really fun.* He not only dreamed up the idea of sex but also designed the equipment for sex. Sex is the result of God's creativity.

The Puritans would have us believe that sex was created by God first and foremost for the purpose of procreation. I don't think so. When we look at Genesis 2:24, the verse about becoming "one flesh," which is a description of the first sex act, it seems God had pleasure in mind. Of course, that pleasurable experience might result in procreation, but pleasure was (and is) the primary purpose of sex.

Sex is a marvelous gift from God that comes with only one instruction: use as directed. And the only direction God gives us about sex is this: sex is to occur only within the marriage relationship. That's the only restriction God gives about the sexual relationship. Do whatever you like to do. Have all the fun you want, but sex is reserved for the marriage relationship. Outside the marriage bond, sex by married men or women is adultery—and God abhors that.[2]

God is pro-sex (within marriage) and anti-adultery. In Malachi 2:13–14, God had this charge against the Israelites: "You cover the altar of the LORD with tears, with weeping and with groaning, because He no longer regards the offering or accepts it with favor from your hand. Yet you say, 'For what reason?' Because the LORD has been a witness between you and the wife of your youth, against whom you have dealt treacherously, though she is your companion and your wife by covenant."

For a man to divorce his wife for another person, for a woman to leave her husband for another person, is to break a covenant relationship. And God treats that very seriously. He said to Israel, in essence, "I will no longer hear your prayers. I will no longer receive your offering because you have dealt with your mate, your covenant partner in life, in a treacherous way."

For a Christian to commit adultery is an unspeakable act. It's an affront against almighty God. God says sex is for the marriage relationship alone. And to deal with your spouse treacherously by committing adultery or leaving your spouse for another person is also an affront to God.

Adultery is a violation of the seventh commandment: "You shall not commit adultery" (Exod. 20:14). However, there's more going on in the seventh commandment than what appears on the surface.

What's Implied and What's Prohibited

Like the sixth commandment (and the eighth commandment), the seventh commandment in the original Hebrew is just two words: *Lo naaph*—"No adultery." But as we saw in the previous chapter on murder, that simple two-word command is deceptively complex. It's equally true with the command against adultery. There's an underlying implication and an expressed prohibition.

The Implication

What's implied is *marriage should be kept holy*—yours and others'. Why does the Bible speak so vehemently against adultery? One reason is that there is probably no relationship that mirrors our relationship with God more than our relationship with our mate. How you treat your mate, in many ways, especially in your fidelity, will determine how you treat God. Marriage is a covenant. It's a sacred relationship.

Paul wrote in 1 Corinthians 7:2, "Each man is to have his own wife, and each woman is to have her own husband." The Greek word translated "have" (*echo*) was used in nonbiblical Greek as a euphemism for *having* another person sexually. Paul couldn't be any clearer: we're not allowed to have sex with someone else's wife or husband.

The teaching of 1 Corinthians 7:2 is one reason that adultery is inexcusable. It's like a rich thief who steals when he has no need to steal. He does it for the thrill of it—and because he can.

But the writer of the book of Hebrews said, "Marriage is to be held in honor among all, and the marriage bed is to be undefiled; for fornicators and adulterers God will judge" (13:4). The bond of marriage is held together by loving fellowship and lifelong faithfulness. Paul admonished husbands to love their wives in the same manner Jesus loved His bride, the church (Eph. 5:25), which is to say, to remain faithful to the point of sacrificing their lives (as Jesus did) for their wives.

The Prohibition

What's prohibited in this commandment is that *married men and women shouldn't defile their bodies*. The prime mover of any sexual sin, including adultery, is lust. James is unmistakable on this point: "Let no one say when he is tempted, 'I am being tempted by God'; for God cannot be tempted by evil, and He Himself does not tempt anyone. But each one is tempted when he is carried away and enticed by *his own lust*. Then when lust has conceived, it gives birth to sin; and when sin is accomplished, it brings forth death" (1:13–15).

James described three downward steps. Applied to adultery, it looks like this: First, we commit *mental adultery* whenever we fantasize about having sex with another man or woman. That's the part about being carried away and enticed to the point that sin is conceived in our minds. This goes to the heart of what Jesus said in Matthew 5:28—and it applies to women just as much as men: "Everyone who looks at a woman with lust for her has already committed adultery with her in his heart."[3] It's the "lust of the eyes" John warned against in 1 John 2:16 that sees a person who is off-limits as an object to be desired and consumed sexually.

Second, we commit *physical adultery* whenever we give in to our mental adultery. This is the part of James's warning in which sin is conceived in our bodies. When this happens, the Lord said we've "committed villainy" (Jer. 29:23 KJV), something wicked and lawless. In fact, Job came right out and said adultery is criminal. He called it a "heinous crime" (31:11 KJV), something odious for which we should be ashamed.

The crime of adultery is committed against innocent spouses. Trust has been severed and real harm done. Adultery sows discord, pitting husband against wife and wife against husband. As a friend has written, "Sexual intercourse is not merely the joining of two bodies for the duration of the act. It entails the whole person—body, soul, and spirit. It's an investment of emotions and wills. Sex is the most intimate experience two people can engage in with each other." In that way, he said, adultery "is a form of theft, stealing . . . from their spouses (to whom a spouse's body belongs)."[4]

The crime is also against God. When Mrs. Potiphar tried and tried and tried again to seduce Joseph, he refused her, not only because having sex with a married woman would be a crime against her husband, his master (Gen. 39:8–9), but also because it would be a crime against God. "How then could I do this great evil and sin against God?" he said (v. 9). David recognized the same thing after his sin with Bathsheba: "Against You, You only, I have sinned and done what is evil in Your sight" (Ps. 51:4).

In 1 Corinthians 6:19–20, Paul said, "Do you not know that your body is a temple of the Holy Spirit who is in you, whom you have from God, and that you are not your own? For you have been bought with a price: therefore glorify God in your body." When a Christian has sex outside of marriage, that believer is taking their body, which belongs to God, and unlawfully giving it to someone else. Therefore, my friend concluded, adultery "is a form of theft, stealing from God (to whom the body belongs)."[5]

But it's worse than that because adultery is more than stealing. Members of the body of Christ, Christians, who join their bodies with a body that doesn't belong to them (through the covenant of marriage) involve the Lord in their illicit act. So repulsive was this thought Paul cried out *me genoito*—"May it never be!" (v. 15).

Finally, the crime is against the adulterer. The apostle Paul made this point clear: "Every other sin that a man commits is outside the body, but the immoral man sins against his own body" (v. 18). Let me quote my friend one last time: "No sin is as directly destructive to the sinner as is the sin of sexual immorality. . . . Other sins such as gluttony and drunkenness encompass morally neutral things, such as food and drink, in which the body participates and, though destructive, can be corrected through abstinence. However, touch can never be untouched; kiss can never be un-kissed; embrace can never be un-embraced. In this sense, all other sins are 'outside of the body,' while sexual sin is 'against [the body]' (6:18)—the body that has become the 'temple of the Holy Spirit,' the indwelling gift from God (6:19)."[6]

Third, when we commit the sin of adultery, we experience *death*, just as James wrote: "when sin is accomplished, it brings forth death" (1:15). James was referring to physical death, which is the penalty all pay for sin (Gen. 2:17; 3:19; Rom. 6:23). But there's more than physical death involved. The sin of adultery might also bring forth the death of a marriage, a family, and a home.

Adultery Destroys and Damns

Adultery is certainly like theft, stealing from God what belongs to Him, stealing from innocent spouses what belongs to them, and, in a way, stealing from yourself what belongs to you—a clear conscience, trust and respect from others, and if not dealt with, potentially your relationships with your spouse and your children.

Adultery carries with it terrible consequences, robbing you not only of the things I've just mentioned but also robbing you of resources. An adulterous affair, particularly one that's ongoing, is an expensive proposition. Warning his son to stay away from the door of an adulterous woman, Solomon said, "Do not desire her beauty in your heart, nor let her capture you with her eyelids. For on account of a harlot one is reduced to a loaf of bread" (Prov. 6:25–26).

These should be enough to deter us from "[drinking] our fill of love" and "[delighting] ourselves with caresses" in the arms of another person (7:18). But they aren't. So here are some other things to contemplate before going too far down the path of lust.

Adultery debases you. In a way, adultery dehumanizes you. In Jeremiah 5:8, the Lord said the adulterer is little better than an animal: "They were well-fed lusty horses, each one neighing after his neighbor's wife." The one consumed by sexual lust loses all sense of reason and reflects a "depraved mind" (Rom. 1:28). The adulterer forgets God and spouse—thinking and acting more like an animal in heat than a reasoning human being.

God also calls the one who becomes an adulterer a walking dunghill—a sewer filled with swill. Proverbs 23:27 says, "A harlot is a deep pit and an adulterous woman [or man] is a narrow well." The idea behind these metaphors—a deep pit and a narrow well—is that they're spaces filled with filth and grime. If you remember the images of Afghan families trying to escape their country in 2021, many of them stood in a sewage ditch that ran alongside the Kabul airport. Adultery is like swimming in that ditch. Shakespeare was right when he penned, "Lust, though to a radiant angel linkt, will sate itself in a celestial bed, and prey on garbage."[7]

Adultery destroys you. The sin of adultery will destroy your body and reputation. Solomon had his share of adulterous affairs, so he knew what he was talking about. Warning his son about adultery, he wrote, "And you groan at your final end, when your flesh and your body are consumed" (5:11). An adulterous relationship can result in diseases, some of which can deform and bring death.

That's how adultery destroys the body. Here's how it destroys your reputation: "A man who commits adultery has no sense; whoever does so destroys himself. Blows and disgrace are his lot, and his shame will never be wiped away" (6:32–33 NIV). If the affair is found out, even if it's forgiven, there's an asterisk by your name. What if a child is produced from the affair? Will you compound the crime and shame with an abortion, or will you give birth to a child who could serve as a constant reminder of your infidelity?

Adultery judges and damns you. Adultery in ancient Israel carried with it a penalty of death, usually by stoning, for both the man and the woman (Lev. 20:10; Deut. 22:24). When a woman caught in adultery was brought before Jesus, those who caught her in the act picked up stones to hurl at her. But before they did, they wanted Jesus's ruling on the matter. Jesus wrote in the dirt and then said to the men, "He who is without sin among you, let him be the first to throw a stone at her" (John 8:7). I believe He recorded the names of the men who stood with stones and jotted down next to each name his own sin. But Jesus didn't dispute the charge against the woman; He chose to show mercy. We see both mercy and judgment in His statement to her. "I do not condemn you"—that's mercy. "Go. From now on sin no more"—that's judgment (v. 11).

The apostles also condemned adultery, stating that sexual immorality is under divine judgment (1 Cor. 6:9–10; Heb. 13:4; 2 Pet. 2:9–10). Therefore, the apostles offered a warning. Adulterous believers should repent, break off their sinful relationship, and work to restore a right relationship with their spouse. Adulterous unbelievers face damnation. By continually giving in to their wanton lusts, living to please their flesh, they demonstrate their unbelief in Jesus Christ and their prideful persistence that they're lords of their own lives. The persistent adulterers' belief that they're free to do whatever with their bodies and the bodies of others, no matter who gets hurt, traps them in a cycle of sin they can never break on their own. Solomon wrote about this in Ecclesiastes 7:26: "I discovered more bitter than death the [adulterous] woman whose heart is *snares* and *nets*, whose hands are *chains*. . . . The sinner will be *captured* by her."

What I left out of that quote, however, was this encouraging word: "One who is pleasing to God will escape from her." Adultery has no place in the lives of believers, who have been saved by the blood of Jesus Christ through faith. If we are pleasing to the Lord, we'll harden our resolve against sinful pleasures. Paul wrote, "Set your mind on the things above, not on the things that are on earth . . . consider the members of your earthly body as dead to immorality, impurity, passion, [and] evil desire" (Col. 3:2, 5). But if you're a Christian who has fallen into the trap of adultery, you can escape—if you soften your heart and seek God's forgiveness through confession and repentance.

Guard Your Heart and Run for Your Life

Before Solomon allowed his heart to be captured and turned from God because of His sexual appetites, he wrote, "Watch over your heart with all diligence, for from it flow the springs of life" (Prov. 4:23). Jesus made a similar observation in Matthew 15: "Out of the heart come evil thoughts, murders, adulteries, fornications, thefts, false witness, slanders" (v. 19). Thinking about sin makes a way for the act of sin. Suppress the first and avoid the second. So *guard your heart* by placing five sentries at your heart's door.

First, *make a covenant with your eyes.* In my book *18 Minutes with Jesus,* I said, "Adultery in the bed begins with adultery in the head."[8] In truth, adultery begins before the head or bed. It begins with the eye, which triggers the lust mechanism in the head (or heart). That's the point of what Jesus said: "Everyone who *looks* at a woman with lust for her has already committed adultery" (5:28). Seeing can lead to sinning; looking can lead to lusting. This was true of Eve. "When the woman *saw* that the tree was good for food, and that it was a *delight to the eyes* . . . she took from its fruit and ate" (Gen. 3:6). It's equally true of false prophets and teachers who "[have] *eyes full of adultery* that never cease from sin, enticing unstable souls" (2 Pet. 2:14). Pornography, which promises sexual gratification without vulnerability or commitment, is especially pernicious because it feasts first on the eyes and then on the mind.

The remedy is to correct your vision by making a covenant with your eyes, as Job did. In defending his integrity from the accusation of three so-called friends, Job said, "I made a covenant with my eyes not to look lustfully at a young woman" (31:1 NIV). We ought to do the same, vowing not to put before our eyes television, movie, or internet images that might cause us to think thoughts we shouldn't think. We ought to make it clear to our spouses that they have permission to check our cell phones and computers at any time, without asking.

Guard your heart by making a covenant with your eyes.

Second, *avoid compromising company.* Paul couldn't have been clearer on this point: "Do not be deceived: 'Bad company corrupts good morals'" (1 Cor. 15:33). Bad characters corrupt the good more than good characters cleanse the bad.

That's why the psalmist said, "How blessed is the man who does not walk in the counsel of the wicked, nor stand in the path of sinners, nor sit in the seat of scoffers!" (Ps. 1:1). Like rust, corruption is silent, slow, and subtle. It begins casually ("walk"), proceeds to curiosity ("stand"), and ends with cooperation ("sit").

Applying this to adultery, it begins with a casual glance as you walk by a coworker's office or cubicle. After a while, glances proceed to standing in their office or by their cubicle, engaging in intimate conversation and flirtation, and maybe having coffee or lunch together. When it becomes clear you have feelings for this person, you entertain thoughts of a more intimate relationship. Finally, it proceeds to a full-blown affair.

If you find yourself somewhere on the spectrum of walking or standing close to an affair, then you need to change course. Find a different route to the breakroom or bathroom. Work different hours or from your home, if possible. Do whatever it takes to avoid the other person. If you find yourself on the brink of an adulterous relationship or in one, break it off immediately. Confess your sin and reconcile with your spouse. And if need be—and I know this is radical—quit your job and find other employment. Your marriage and family are more important than your bank account.

Guard your heart by avoiding compromising company.

Third, *watch your time*. The Living Bible paraphrases Proverbs 16:27 in a way that has become a cliché but is nonetheless true: "Idle hands are the devil's workshop; idle lips are his mouthpiece." Leisure gives us time to listen to temptation and license to lie in a bed of sin "sprinkled . . . with myrrh, aloes and cinnamon," as Solomon put it (7:17). We see this with David and his sin with Bathsheba. Instead of being in the field with his army, David lounged around Jerusalem—bored. One evening, while "[walking] around on the roof [of his palace] . . . he saw a woman bathing; and the woman was very beautiful" (2 Sam. 11:2). He wanted to know who she was. Turns out, she was the granddaughter of an adviser, the daughter of a mighty man, and the wife of an elite soldier (v. 3). None of that mattered to David. He wanted her and he would have her, so he took her (v. 4). For David, his one night of pleasure brought a lifetime of pain—the death of the child conceived that night, a war, the incestuous rape of his daughter, and never-ending trouble with his eldest son.[9] All that for one night of forbidden passion. Too much time on your hands gives the devil an opportunity to take those idle hands and turn them into adulterous hands.

Guard your heart by watching your time.

Fourth, *desire your spouse*. If ever a hypocrite lived, Solomon, with his seven hundred wives and three hundred concubines, was the embodiment of hypocrisy, particularly in his later years. His was a "Do as I say, not as I do" philosophy. Though he didn't follow his own advice, it's wise advice nonetheless. He told his married son, "Drink water from your own cistern and fresh water from your own well. Should your springs be dispersed abroad, streams of water in the streets? Let them be yours alone and not for strangers with you. Let your fountain be blessed, and rejoice in the wife of your youth. As a loving hind and a graceful doe, let her breasts satisfy you at all times; be exhilarated always with her love. For why should you, my son, be exhilarated with an adulteress and embrace the bosom of a foreigner?" (Prov. 5:15–20).

We can find sexual stimulation either inside or outside of marriage. God knows that. He includes this highly charged passage in Scripture because He wants to demonstrate His approval of sexual joy and ecstasy—*within the bond of marriage*. Anything else meets with His disapproval. So, in symbolic language, the Lord led Solomon to admonish his son to drink deeply from the fresh, clean waters offered by his wife. However, in my years of ministry I've noticed that men and women often grow tired of drinking from the same fountain. They become deluded into thinking that someone else's fountain will offer something better—water that is sweeter tasting or maybe has added fizz. What they fail to notice, until it's too late, is that drinking from someone else's fountain is like drinking from a muddy drainage ditch.

To keep us at our own water fountain, Solomon advised us to "rejoice in the wife [or husband] of [our] youth . . . [being] exhilarated always with her [or his] love." The best way to do that is to invest in your marriage. Date each other again. Find ways to break the bedroom boredom and introduce fun. Share intimate secrets and dreams with each other, and no one else.

Guard your heart by desiring your spouse.

Fifth, *learn to fear God*. The greatest guard for your heart is to fear the Lord. Solomon wrote, "By the fear of the LORD one keeps away from evil" (16:6). This often gets misinterpreted that we should cower in God's presence, like frightened children about to be whacked. But that's not what it means to fear God. It means to stand in awe of Him, to respect Him as a loving Father who won't tolerate disobedience. He might discipline us, but He never disciplines us out of anger and wrath. Rather, God disciplines His children out of love and goodwill (Heb. 12:4–11).

How can you learn to fear the Lord? The best way is to spend time in His presence by spending time in His Word and in prayer. Back in Psalm 1, the "blessed" person who doesn't stroll, stand, or sit with sinners is the one who "[delights] in the law of the LORD" by "[meditating on it] day and night" (v. 2). Later in the psalms, David says "reverence" for God is a byproduct of God, "[establishing His] word" in our hearts (119:38). In Proverbs 7, Solomon instructed his son to call wisdom that comes from God's Word his "sister" and to call understanding his "intimate friend" because "they [will] keep you from an adulteress" (vv. 4–5).

Another way to develop the fear of God is to realize that God is always watching. He never closes his eyes to sleep (Ps. 121:4) but scans the earth looking for those who are faithful to Him (2 Chron. 16:9). Nothing is hidden from His eyes (Heb. 4:13). Solomon said, "The ways of a man are before the eyes of the LORD, and He watches all his paths" (Prov. 5:21). There's no surveillance system sophisticated enough and no form of Big Brother government or technology large enough to outmatch God when it comes to gathering data on you. He not only knows everything you've ever done; He knows every motive behind everything you've ever done. "The LORD weighs the hearts" (21:2), and by His Word He divides soul and spirit, bone and marrow, and is "able to judge the thoughts and intentions of the heart" (Heb. 4:12). That ought to cause you to think twice before climbing into bed with someone other than your spouse.

Guard your heart by learning to fear God.

Let me wrap up this chapter with one final admonition. Paul instructed the Corinthian Christians to "flee immorality" (1 Cor. 6:18). In essence, he said the same thing to Timothy: "Flee from youthful lusts" (2 Tim. 2:22).[10] The one who took such advice to heart, even though he lived thousands of years

before, was Joseph. When Mrs. Potiphar persisted in her se-
duction of Joseph, even trying to force him to sleep with her,
"he left his garment in her hand and fled, and went outside"
(Gen. 39:12).

You can't go toe-to-toe with lust on your own. You don't have
the willpower to resist its allure. So, while you do whatever is
necessary to guard your heart, when lust comes knocking on
your door, *run for your life*. You can't lust if you're running—and
you certainly can't commit adultery when your track shoes
are in motion.

The Eighth Commandment: Respect the Property of Others

8

The Eighth Commandment: Respect the Property of Others

You shall not steal.

Exodus 20:15

None of the parents suspected Sister Mary Margaret Kreuper of any impropriety. Nor could they account for the school's continued shortfall in funds. For twenty-eight years, Sister Mary Margaret had been the beloved principal at St. James Catholic School in Torrance, California. But in 2021, a federal judge sentenced the nun to one year and one day in a federal penitentiary for wire fraud and money laundering. He also ordered her to repay the $835,339 she'd embezzled from school funds—money intended to educate the children placed under her care and to keep the school's facilities clean, safe, and up-to-date. "I have sinned. I have broken the law," the eighty-year-old nun confessed. "I have no excuses."

The judge who tried the case said he struggled in handing down a sentence. But despite her age, her years of service as an educator, and her religious devotion as a nun for sixty-two years, some form of punishment was necessary.[1]

When I read the story of Sister Mary Margaret, the first thing that went through my mind was, *You just never know about people.* The next thing I thought—and this sent a shiver down my spine—was, *What about my financial adviser? After all, if you can't trust a nun with your money, who can you trust?*

Sister Mary Margaret obviously violated United States law. She also violated God's law, which says, "You shall not steal" (Exod. 20:15).

Like the sixth and seventh commandments, the eighth commandment consists of only two words in the original Hebrew: *Lo ganab*—"No stealing." As we'll see, the command is broad in scope. Moses said, "Do not steal. . . . Do not defraud or rob your neighbor. Do not hold back the wages of a hired worker overnight" (Lev. 19:11, 13 NIV).

By issuing the eighth commandment, God implied His approval of private property ownership—and with it, His approval of social order. Just as murder and adultery are detrimental to the common good, so is theft. Without laws to prevent theft and prosecute thieves, there can be no civil society. Anarchy would reign.

That's what some American cities discovered after the 2020 murder of George Floyd by Minneapolis police officers. In the wake of that horrific crime, there were calls for cities to defund the police. Cities like San Francisco and Seattle did just that. What resulted were police forces stretched so thin they couldn't respond to some crimes.

In San Francisco, the police stopped answering shoplifting calls. Crime became rampant, and things became so chaotic that some businesses shut their doors and sent employees home. Other businesses refused to open stores in the city. After a while, certain neighborhoods no longer had drugstores or grocery stores serving their communities. Everything had been stolen, and the businesses were boarded up. Finally, the mayor, who had been in favor of defunding the police, announced that the police budget would be increased and officers would be dispatched to shoplifting calls.[2]

"Power to Make Money"

Theft is rooted in contempt for others.[3] It's the false notion that what's yours ought to be mine, and if I can't get it by any other means, then I'll take it for myself. It's one of three ways we can acquire wealth and gain property. The other two include work and inheritance. Paul identified these three methods in Ephesians 4:28: "He who steals must steal no longer; but rather he must labor, performing with his own hands what is good, so that he will have something to share with one who has need."

The Bible assumes we're going to acquire property. There's nothing wrong with acquiring property or possessions. But the Bible also assumes we're going to acquire those things legitimately, not illegitimately.

Obviously, the most common form of acquiring wealth and property legitimately is to *work for it*—that's the point behind the phrase "he must labor, performing with his own hands what is good." The Lord provides the necessary talents, intellect, and opportunities for everyone committed to working for his or her own property. Moses told the second-generation Israelites who were about to enter the promised land, "Remember the LORD your God, for it is He who is giving you power to make wealth" (Deut. 8:18). This doesn't mean God gives us everything necessary to become billionaires. Rather, He gives us everything necessary to earn a living so we can take care of our own household, just as Paul instructed (2 Thess. 3:10–12; 1 Tim. 5:8).

By the way, work was always part of God's plan for us. Even before the fall, God created human beings to work. God told the first couple, "Be fruitful and multiply, and fill the earth, and *subdue it*; and *rule over* the fish of the sea and over the birds of the sky and over every living thing that moves on the earth" (Gen. 1:28). In other words, we're commanded to serve as overseers or managers of God's creation. Specifically, God placed the first couple in the garden of Eden to tend it: "Then the LORD God took the man and put him into the garden of Eden to cultivate it and keep it" (2:15).

You might remember the Super Bowl commercial from a number of years ago featuring the voice and commentary of Paul Harvey. Against the backdrop of cultivated fields, horses and cattle, and barns and tractors, boomed Harvey's voice: "God said . . . 'I need somebody with arms strong enough to rustle a calf and yet gentle enough to deliver his own grandchild. Somebody to call hogs, tame cantankerous machinery, come home hungry, have to wait lunch until his wife's done feeding visiting ladies and tell the ladies to be sure and come back real soon—and mean it.' So God made a farmer."[4]

That's what He made out of Adam: a farmer, a cultivator of the ground. Unfortunately, after Adam's sin, cultivating the ground—and performing any kind of work—became more difficult, no doubt about it (3:17–19). But hard or not, God intends for us to work for what we get. When we do, we appreciate it more.

I remember my very first car. When I was in high school, my father, who loved to tinker with and rebuild old Volkswagens, gave me a blue Beetle. One day I asked him about the air conditioning. He said, "Well, it has a two-sixty air conditioner." I asked him, "What's that?" He said, "Roll two windows down and go sixty miles an hour and you'll be fine." That Volkswagen was a great car until the fuel line came off and the engine exploded. But as much as I appreciated that car, I had greater appreciation for the first car I purchased with my own money. There's just something satisfying about working for what you get. That's God's plan for acquiring property.

The other means of acquiring wealth and property is to *inherit it*—that's implied in the phrase "so that he will have something to share with one who has need" (Eph. 4:28). Working hard for your money not only to make a living but also to put some away gives you an opportunity to be generous—to help those in immediate need and to leave something behind when you're gone. Solomon, who inherited great wealth from his father, David, said, "A good man leaves an inheritance to his children's children"—his grandchildren (Prov. 13:22). We ought to leave behind the legacy of a good example and a good name, but we should also leave behind something more tangible. In ancient Israel, the ability to bequeath wealth to your grandchildren was the supreme test of a family's ability to prosper generationally.

I recently read about the father of the East Texas oil boom, Columbus Marion "Dad" Joiner. He made and lost two fortunes as a wildcatter in the oil business before hitting it big in 1930, when he struck in Rusk County the largest oil field in the world at that time. However, to finance his drilling operations, Joiner sold and resold the same oil leases to unsuspecting investors. When his well came in and it was time to reimburse his investors, his scheme was discovered, and lawsuits began pouring into the courts. By the early 1940s, Joiner put his company in voluntary receivership and sold his wells and leases to H. L. Hunt for pennies on the dollar. When Joiner died in 1947, his estate was estimated to be three million dollars but was still tied up in legal wrangling. His eight children inherited next to nothing in comparison to the value of the oil sucked from the Texas fields under Joiner's leases.[5]

I don't know if Joiner ever read Acts 20, but if he had, he might have been more careful in how he handled his business to ensure he left an inheritance for his children. In that chapter, Paul reminded the elders of the Ephesian church of his work ethic and diligence in making tents to care for his own needs. He said, "In everything I showed you that by working hard in this manner you must help the weak and remember the words of the Lord Jesus, that He Himself said, 'It is more blessed to give than to receive'" (v. 35). Rest assured, if you inherited property from your family, then someone before you worked hard to earn it. As a follower of Christ, you're under the obligation to work hard to maintain it, protect it, and add to it (if you can) so you can pass it on.

"He Who Steals Must Steal No Longer"

Of course, not everyone wants to work for what they get. And few are fortunate to inherit enough money that they don't need to work. So some turn to stealing.

Contemptuous of others' good fortune—whether through work or inheritance—the thief has a gnawing dissatisfaction with what God provides. Many believe God is holding out on them. As J. I. Packer put it, "Temptations to steal property— that is, to deprive another person of what he or she has a right to—arise because fallen man always, instinctively, wants more than he has at present and more than others have."[6] In other words, the thief covets what isn't theirs (breaking the tenth commandment) and takes it (breaking the eighth commandment).

I've identified four broad categories of how thieves practice their thievery.[7]

Despoiling

First, we violate the eighth commandment whenever we *despoil* someone by breaking into and entering their home, car, or business and carting off their goods. *Despoil* is a word rarely used anymore, but it's perfect for describing simple theft. As theologian John Calvin explained, it's an act of "violence . . . when a man's goods are forcibly plundered and carried off."[8] Chances are a good many of you are victims of this crime. You've been mugged on the street, or some creep has broken into your home, rummaged through your car, or snatched your wallet or phone. Few things are more violating than a stranger stealing your property.

Perhaps all but a handful of you are saying right about now, "This is one of the Ten Commandments I'm not guilty of breaking." Well, hold on there. Not so fast. Just as there's more than one way to skin a cat, as the old saying goes, there's more than one way to despoil someone. Students who cheat on exams are breaking the eighth commandment by the fact that they're "invading" someone else's space and stealing another's answers. Employees who take home office supplies—pens and paper and paper clips—and neighbors who forget to return borrowed items—tools, books, and dishes—have all despoiled others.

We can also despoil someone by stealing their ideas and claiming them as our own. Pastors are some of the worst offenders of this. A few years back, a woman sent an email telling me how much she enjoyed a particular sermon she watched Saturday evening on *Pathway to Victory*, my radio and television ministry, and how much she enjoyed hearing that same sermon—delivered word for word—a second time on the following Sunday by her pastor. He even downloaded the outline of my sermon from the PTV website and handed it out. Now, I don't mind if other pastors borrow ideas or illustrations, or even short quotes, from my sermons. We all borrow from other people. But if you borrow substantially, if you preach a sermon verbatim or quote long passages or have the substance of an idea that comes from someplace else, give people credit for it. To take an entire sermon and preach it as if it were your own—or to download a paper off the internet and pass it off as your own—is the classic definition of despoiling someone, plundering their hard work and intellectual property.

Dishonesty

Second, we violate the eighth commandment whenever we're *dishonest* with someone by lying, manipulating, or flattering them out of their goods. Did you know we have laws regulating weights and measures, to ensure that when you buy a pound of meat or pump a gallon of gas you're getting what you pay for? Dishonesty in the attempt to rob others is an abomination to God. That's why Proverbs 11:1 says, "A false balance is an abomination to the LORD, but a just weight is His delight."[9]

I've seen funny videos showing someone standing on a bathroom scale while a spouse or child places a toe on the scale to throw off the weight. That isn't what the Lord is warning against. Nor is the warning simply against imbalanced scales. It can be applied to any form of dishonesty where the intention is to take advantage of someone to their material loss.

For example, the classic illustration of dishonesty is the used car salesperson. But theft through dishonesty has become more sophisticated in the internet age. You probably get your share of "phishing" emails notifying you that your bank account is overdrawn or you're late on a payment or your Amazon order didn't go through. Each of these emails asks you to click on a link and provide certain personal information such as a bank account number or your Social Security number. It's all a lie. But if they get your information, they can steal your identity or clean out your account by making charges in your name without ever physically breaking into your home or robbing your bank.

Defrauding

Third, we violate the eighth commandment whenever we *defraud* someone by not paying them what we owe. Biblically, this takes on three applications.

The first way we defraud others is by *failing to pay our debts*. In Proverbs 3:27–28, Solomon wrote, "Do not withhold good from those to whom it is due, when it is in your power to do it. Do not say to your neighbor, 'Go, and come back, and tomorrow I will give it.'" The point is, when we have debts to pay, and we have the money to pay them, we should pay promptly. If we don't, we not only defraud the one to whom the debt is owed but also defraud others not party to our transactions. How is that? Well, there's a reason we pay outrageous percentage points on credit cards and bank loans. Whenever someone defaults on their debt and files for bankruptcy, the creditor doesn't just eat that loss; they pass it to their other customers, who pay for the default in higher interest rates. Don't get me wrong; things happen in life that are sometimes out of our control, throwing us into a financial tailspin. But many who could pay something on their debts choose not to. They'd rather defraud their creditors by defaulting, thereby stealing from them and others.

There are others who underreport or refuse to pay their taxes. That's fraud and thievery because they enjoy the benefits of living in a civilized country without supporting the institutions that keep that country civilized. I know the government isn't perfect, and some of our tax dollars support initiatives I don't agree with. And though I pray the rapture will come every April 14, I also know I'm under the command of Christ to "render to Caesar the things that are Caesar's" (Matt. 22:21) on April 15.

The second way we can defraud someone and steal from them is *not giving an employer 100 percent during the workweek and not giving an employee what is owed.* That's the concern Paul had in Colossians 3 and 4. To employees, Paul said, "In all things obey those who are [over you] on earth, not with external service, as those who merely please men, but with sincerity of heart, fearing the Lord. Whatever you do, do your work heartily, as for the Lord rather than for men, knowing that from the Lord you will receive the reward of the inheritance. It is the Lord Christ whom you serve" (3:22–24). When employees don't put in a full day's work for a full day's pay, they're guilty of thievery, defrauding their employer of what is due.

But employers can also defraud their employees. That's what Paul took up in Colossians 4: "[Employers], grant to your [employees] justice and fairness, knowing that you too have a Master in heaven" (v. 1). A friend of mine used to work for someone who required salaried employees to sign in if they were late to work. If it happened too often the employee could be disciplined—a dressing down by a manager or a dock in time off. However, it was looked down upon if an employee signed out after they had worked more than an eight-hour day. If an employee worked overtime, they weren't compensated for the extra hours since everyone was salaried. To dock someone without also compensating them for extra hours was a way for the company to squeeze out extra dollars by squeezing employees, and that's a violation of the eighth commandment.

The third way we can defraud someone is *stealing from God*. "Whoa, there, Pastor," I can hear some of you say. "How can I steal from God?" Good question. It's the same question God asked in Malachi 3. Can you imagine pulling a gun and thrusting it in God's face, saying, "Stick 'em up—give me Your money"? It doesn't happen like that, but God is clear: "You are robbing Me! . . . In tithes and offerings" (v. 8). The Hebrew word for "rob" (*qaba*) in this passage is the word for *defraud*. The ancient Israelites were commanded to give a tenth of their yield to the work of God, to support the temple and the priesthood (Lev. 27:30). The tithe belongs to the Lord. And when we withhold what belongs to God, that's the same as robbing God.

Tithing isn't specifically mentioned in the New Testament, but the idea of giving to the Lord and His work—and giving generously—is. In 2 Corinthians 9, Paul admonished believers to fulfill their promise to give to God, and not to do it "grudgingly or under compulsion," but openly and freely because "God loves a cheerful giver" (v. 7). Anything short of blessing God with your giving, with the blessings He's given to you, is defrauding God and stealing from Him.

Defaming

Fourth, we violate the eighth commandment whenever we *defame* someone by spreading slander and gossip with the intent of stealing their good name. We'll look at this in greater detail in chapter 9, so I'll not spend much time here, but defaming someone is a form of theft because it robs them of their reputation. In his play *Othello*, William Shakespeare put into the mouth of Iago these words: "Who steals my purse steals trash; 'tis something, nothing. . . . But he that filches from me my good name robs me of that which not enriches him and makes me poor indeed."[10] Defamation is a violation of the eighth commandment, and it's the reason Paul said, "Put . . . aside: anger, wrath, malice, *slander*, and abusive speech from your mouth" (Col. 3:8).

"Not Ashamed on the Day of Judgment"

Whenever we steal from others we're also stealing from ourselves, robbing ourselves of one of life's most important gifts: a clear conscience. Writing to his protégé, Timothy, Paul said the purpose of his instruction "is love from a pure heart and a good conscience and a sincere faith" (1 Tim. 1:5). When a pastor instructs his people, he is to make sure that his emotional and volitional core has been sanctified by Christ, that his thinking and decision-making process has been made holy by Christ, and that his life of faith reflects the active and authentic nature of Christ. That's why the old apostle encouraged the young pastor to keep the "faith and a good conscience, which some have rejected and suffered shipwreck in regard to their faith" (v. 19).

Do you know what a clear conscience is? It's the ability to look yourself in the mirror without shame or guilt, to look someone in the eye knowing they can't accuse you of wrongdoing or a wrong that you haven't attempted to make right. Can you do that? Can you look yourself in the mirror or look someone in the eye without blushing or diverting your gaze? Can you honestly say you've never despoiled someone, been dishonest to the point of thievery, defrauded someone of their money, or defamed them by robbing them of their good name? If you answered no to any of those questions, then you need to make things right. We'll look at this in more detail in the next section, but you need to make restitution—to pay back what you've taken with interest.

I love the story of David (Davy) Crockett before he came to Texas, when he was a sophomore congressman from Tennessee. During the legislative session of 1829–30, one of the primary goals of newly elected president Andrew Jackson was the passage of the Indian Removal Act, which required all southeastern American Indians to abandon their homelands and resettle in what was then called "Indian Territory"— present-day Oklahoma. The trek became known as the Trail of Tears, not only because of the loss of tribal lands but also because so many American Indians died along the way.

Jackson was a Tennessean, as was Crockett, so it was understood that Crockett would not only vote for the bill but would champion it before the House of Representatives. He did neither. Here's what he said about it:

> It was expected of me that I was to bow to the name of Andrew Jackson, and follow him in all his motions, and mindings, and turnings, even at the expense of my conscience and judgment. Such a thing was new to me.... His famous, or rather I should say his in-*famous*, Indian bill was brought forward, and I opposed it from the purest motives in the world. Several of my colleagues got around me, and told me how well they loved me, and that I was ruining myself. They said this was a favourite measure of the president, and I ought to go for it. I told them I believed it was a wicked, unjust measure, and that I should go against it, let the cost to myself be what it might.... I voted against this Indian bill, and my conscience yet tells me that I gave a good honest vote, one that I believe will not make me ashamed on the day of judgment.[11]

Crockett finished out that term and promptly lost reelection. Afterward, he left Tennessee for Texas, where he fought and died for Texas independence, dying with a clear conscience, knowing he didn't despoil or defraud American Indians of their lands.

"Give Back Four Times as Much"

When it comes to the topic of theft, it isn't enough simply to confess our crimes, even if our theft isn't criminal in the legal sense. Confession is merely a first step. The Lord also requires us to make restitution to right the wrong we've committed, which is intended to serve as a deterrent to continual theft on our part and to anyone tempted to steal from others.

Because God places more value on human life and human relationships than He does on material possessions, the penalty for theft in ancient Israel was less severe than it was for murder or adultery. For them, depending on whether the theft was due to negligent and careless loss of a neighbor's property, defrauding a neighbor, or outright stealing, restitution usually fell under a five-to-one, four-to-one, or two-to-one ratio.[12]

For example, if a thief stole an ox and either slaughtered or sold it, he was required to pay back the owner five oxen. If the thief stole a sheep and either slaughtered or sold it, he was required to pay back the owner four sheep (Exod. 22:1). However, if the ox or sheep was found alive, then the thief was required to return the animal and pay back the owner double (v. 4). If money was stolen, then the thief had to pay back the original sum and double it (v. 7).

The act of restitution is played out beautifully in the New Testament in the life of the tax collector Zaccheus. Tax collectors in Israel at the time were Jews who made a business arrangement with the Roman government to collect taxes on the state's behalf. Luke tells us Zaccheus was the "chief tax collector" in the district of Jericho and "was rich" (19:2). Zaccheus's wealth wasn't derived from his salary as a civil servant but from the common practice among tax collectors of padding their pockets by overcharging the people. Abusing their power, tax collectors took not only the state-mandated amounts but more than what the state required. The extra went directly into the tax collector's purse.

Since Zaccheus was the chief tax collector, managing other tax collectors, he received a cut of the extra money they collected in a sort of first-century pyramid scheme.

Zaccheus was considered by other Jews as a traitor and thief, and he was viewed with contempt—but not by Jesus. Zaccheus had heard of Jesus and wanted to see Him as He passed through Jericho on His way to Jerusalem. "Small in stature," Zaccheus climbed a sycamore tree to see over the crowd that had gathered (vv. 3–4). While passing by the tree, Jesus looked up and called Zaccheus by name, inviting Himself to stay the night in Zaccheus's house, which Zaccheus gladly accepted (vv. 5–6).

When the people saw Jesus entering Zaccheus's house, they began to "grumble" (v. 7), but Zaccheus humbled himself. He pledged to give half his estate to support the poor and to make restitution, up to "four times as much," of anyone he defrauded (v. 8).

Jesus interpreted Zaccheus's pledge as a confession of faith, understanding that Zaccheus had confessed to the sin of idolatry (worshiping money and violating the first commandment) and thievery (extorting money from others and violating the eighth commandment). Such a confession could come only from a heart of faith. That's why Jesus declared, "Today salvation has come to this house" (v. 9).

Now, as "a son of Abraham" (v. 9), Zaccheus could enter into the full covenant blessing promised to Abraham and his faithful descendants. Salvation, like Zaccheus's, was the reason that Jesus came—"to seek and to save that which was lost" (v. 10).

Theft is an act of injustice and "is an abomination to the LORD your God" (Deut. 25:16). So to ensure you gain and maintain a clear conscience—and to please the Lord who came to save you from the sins of idolatry, coveting, and stealing—I challenge you to search your heart to determine whether you have a little larceny residing there. If so, then I challenge you to repent and make restitution—and to do it now.

The Ninth Commandment:
Protect the Reputation
of Others

9

The Ninth Commandment: Protect the Reputation of Others

You shall not bear false witness against your neighbor.

Exodus 20:16

Politicians lie. There's nothing new or surprising about that. It's the rare politician indeed who, if asked if they lie, would come right out and tell the truth. At best, they might admit to what Winston Churchill called "terminological inexactitude."[1]

However, the question isn't whether politicians lie. The question is, Do you lie? Are you known as a truth-teller or a teller of tall tales? Do you engage in "terminological inexactitude"? To find out, let's hook you up to a mental lie detector. As honestly as possible, answer the following questions:

1. Do you have a secret life you don't want others to discover?
2. You're browsing in an antique shop and accidentally knock over an expensive vase. Do you tell the owner and pay for the damages?
3. Would you agree to answer any question your spouse asked you if you were hooked up to an actual lie detector?
4. Do you often say things you don't mean for the sake of politeness?
5. Have you ever lied about your age, education, or income?
6. Would you tell a close friend that he or she had bad breath?
7. Have you ever said "I love you" without meaning it?
8. Would you give your spouse the password to your computer and/or cell phone?
9. Do you really love and respect your in-laws?
10. Did you lie on this test?

How did you do? If you were honest, you've probably lied in one or more of the scenarios on this list. If so, you've broken the ninth commandment: "You shall not bear false witness against your neighbor" (Exod. 20:16).

We'll spend time examining what the ninth commandment means, but before we do, let me point out something: as with the three previous commandments, the ninth commandment has to do with taking something from your neighbor. We could summarize commandments six and seven like this: don't take your neighbor's life or wife, and commandments eight and nine like this: don't take your neighbor's goods or good name. It's interesting that the ninth commandment deals with lying because those who commit murder, adultery, and theft are all adept at terminological inexactitude.

As with commandments six and seven, dealing with murder and adultery, the ninth commandment gives us an extreme example of sinning, but it also covers lesser forms of falsehoods, which we will take up first.[2]

Comments about Lying, Generally

When talking about lying, it's helpful to remember the difference between telling an unknown falsehood and telling a known falsehood. Not everyone who passes on an untruth is an intentional liar. Many times people are duped into believing (and spreading) things that just aren't so. We see this all the time when people forward emails or share social media posts that turn out to be fake news. We might accuse them of not doing their homework to ferret out the truth, lacking discernment and being gullible enough to be taken in by a charlatan, or being stubborn in their refusal to listen to competing voices. However, that doesn't necessarily make them liars, even though the things they say may be lies, because they might say these things unknowingly or foolishly.

Liars, on the other hand, know exactly what they're doing: contradicting the truth. Their motive is to spread disinformation, half-truths (which, according to a Yiddish proverb, is a whole lie), fabrications, fake news, and untruths. They intend to deceive, like the mother who boarded a train with her six-year-old son. The train company charged fares only for those six and up, so the mother instructed her son to tell the conductor he was five years old when the conductor came around punching tickets. Sure enough, when the conductor reached the boy, the conductor asked, "How old are you, son?" The boy said, "Ah, five." The boy's mother didn't have to pay his fare. After finishing his rounds, the conductor came back through the car where the boy and mother sat. He paused and asked the boy, "How are you enjoying the train ride?" "I like it," the boy said. "Great. So when are you gonna be six?" The boy answered, "About the time I get off this train."[3]

Generally, children don't like lying for their parents. God isn't too keen on the idea either, which is why He says we shouldn't do it. In the book of Proverbs, there are a number of verses I think everyone should memorize because they distill the truth into a few punchy points. Do you remember the former talk-show host David Letterman's famous "top ten" lists? Well, God has His "top seven" list of sins He hates the most, and it's found in Proverbs 6:16–19. Solomon wrote in verse 16, "There are six things which the LORD hates, yes, seven which are an abomination to Him." Then, in verses 17–19, Solomon laid out the list like a deck of cards:

1. "Haughty eyes."
2. "A lying tongue."
3. "Hands that shed innocent blood."
4. "A heart that devises wicked plans."[4]
5. "Feet that run rapidly to evil."
6. "A false witness who utters lies."[5]
7. "One who spreads strife among brothers."[6]

Did you notice out of the seven things that God hates most, two of them have to do with lying? A lying tongue (v. 17) and a false witness who utters lies (v. 19). It's clear that God hates lying.

To demonstrate just how much God hates the spreading of falsehoods, all we need to do is look at something that happened in the first church at Jerusalem. During that time it was common for believers to pool their resources, since Christians were a minority and Jews who came to believe in Jesus as Messiah were sometimes persecuted and had their livelihoods taken from them. One man in particular who wanted to make sure members of the Jerusalem church were provided for was a man named Joseph, though we know him as Barnabas, which means "Son of Encouragement" (Acts 4:36). He owned some real estate that he sold. He then brought the proceeds to the church to be distributed as people had need (v. 37).

I suspect Barnabas didn't make a show of his gift but gave it in secret. As often happens in churches, rumors spread about this generosity. Not to be outdone, a couple named Ananias and Sapphira, who also owned property, sold it and gave the proceeds to the church. But instead of donating 100 percent of the value, they gave only a portion of the proceeds, which would've been fine. The profit from the property was theirs to do with as they liked. However, what wasn't fine was the fact that they lied about their gift. They told the apostles their donation represented the total amount of the proceeds, when it didn't (5:1–2). For what Peter called "[lying] to the Holy Spirit," the Lord struck Ananias dead (vv. 3–6). Not knowing what had happened to her husband, Sapphira stopped by the church later that day and ran into Peter, who confronted her about the money with the same result—she lied and died (vv. 7–10).

The outcome of what happened to Ananias and Sapphira is found in verse 11: "And great fear came over the whole church, and over all who heard of these things." That's one of the greatest understatements in the whole Bible. A friend told me after reading this passage that Peter missed a golden opportunity. If he'd passed the basket right then, he would've taken in the largest offering in the history of the church! That's how we preachers sometimes think. But that's not how God thinks, not about lying.

"But, Pastor," I can hear you saying, "what about Rahab?" You may remember her story from the book of Joshua.[7] Rahab was a prostitute who lived in Jericho; nevertheless, she believed God had ordained that the Israelites would be victorious over Jericho. Joshua sent spies into Jericho to case the city, and they found refuge in Rahab's home. When the king of Jericho sent word asking about these spies, Rahab lied. She told them that they had left when, in fact, she was hiding them (Josh. 2:1–7). People say, "Now, wait a minute. Why did Rahab make God's hall of fame in Hebrews 11? Does God commend lying?" Well, the answer is of course not. What Rahab is commended for in Hebrews 11:31 is not her lying but her faith. She believed that God was going to fulfill His promise to Israel. She was willing to risk her life to see that promise fulfilled, and that's what God honored, not her lying.

Why God Hates Lying

The Bible is clear that lying is one of those sins the Lord hates—and I can think of two reasons.

First, God hates lying because of its *origin*. Jesus's half brother James reminded us that God is "the Father of lights, with whom there is no variation or shifting shadow" (1:17). In other words, God is absolute truth; He is the very definition or essence of truth. In fact, Paul said in Titus 1:2 that God "cannot lie."[8]

On the other hand, Satan is the very definition or essence of lies. Jesus couldn't make it plainer when He said that the devil "does not stand in the truth because there is no truth in him. Whenever he speaks a lie, he speaks from his own nature, for he is a liar and the father of lies" (John 8:44).

So whenever Christians tell lies, we're acting more like children of Satan than children of God. Lying is contrary to who we are—brothers and sisters of Jesus Christ. As theologian J. I. Packer wrote, "There is no godliness without truthfulness."[9] The apostle Paul said, "Lay aside the old self, which is being corrupted in accordance with the lusts of deceit . . . and put on the new self, which in the likeness of God has been created in righteousness and holiness of the truth. Therefore, laying aside falsehood, speak truth each one of you with his neighbor, for we are members of one another" (Eph. 4:22, 24–25). God hates lying because it didn't originate with Him but with Satan.

Second, God hates lying because of its *outcome*. The King James Version of Proverbs 6:19 equates liars with sowing discord in the family of God. I had a deacon in my first church in Eastland, Texas, who used to say, "God hates those who sow *discourse* among brethren." He could never get the right word—"discord." The Lord hates those who cause trouble and bring division in the church, in the family, or among friends. And lying is the primary vehicle for doing that. Most people would say the number one quality valued above all others in a friendship is honesty. I bet if you looked back over your relationships that turned sour, you would find that deceit or some form of untruth was at the heart of the breakup. Lying causes division among people.

Ways in Which We Lie

Just as there's more than one way to commit adultery or murder or steal, there's more than one way to lie. I've identified four of them.

Contradicting the Truth

First, we lie by knowingly *contradicting the truth*. We lie when we say something that's absolutely contrary to truth. This was the basis of the first lie, told in the garden of Eden by Satan himself. God instructed Adam, "From any tree in the garden you may eat freely; but from the tree of the knowledge of good and evil you shall not eat, for in the day that you eat from it you will surely die" (Gen. 2:16–17). Adam, no doubt, passed that truth on to Eve. However, when Satan approached Eve (in the guise of a serpent), he contradicted the truth of God's Word, saying, "You surely will not die!" (3:4). We know what happened. Eve and Adam (v. 6) believed the lie, acted on it, and were punished with death (v. 19). We live with the outcome of that lie to this day (Rom. 5:12).

Why do people engage in lying today?[10] Sometimes we contradict the truth because we want to impress people. We pretend to be someone we're not or pretend that our circumstances are different than they actually are, hoping people will like us more.

Sometimes we contradict the truth because we want to seek revenge by spreading lies about others. Maybe somebody has hurt us, so we choose to get back at them by spreading information we know is false. Social media has become a useful tool for that. Sometimes we contradict the truth to escape the consequences of our actions, like lying to a police officer in hopes of getting out of a speeding ticket.

Sometimes we contradict the truth to keep from hurting other people's feelings, so we say things we don't mean. Maybe someone invites us to do something we don't want to do, so we make up some excuse.

Sometimes we contradict the truth simply because it's convenient. Years ago, I preached about telling the truth. While driving home from church, I was trying to impress on my daughters the importance of applying their daddy's sermon. My older daughter, Julia, who was about eight at the time, said, "Oh, is that like when somebody calls home and Mom answers the phone and you tell her to say you're not there?"

But enough about me.

Twisting the Truth

A second way in which we lie is by knowingly *twisting the truth*. Sometimes distortions of the truth are more dangerous than outright lies because there's just enough veracity in the distortion to make it seem plausible. Preacher and teacher Calvin Miller wrote about a time when he was in seminary and working the night shift in a factory. He had fallen behind on studying for a final exam and needed the night off to study, but he didn't think his boss would give it to him. He didn't want to out-and-out lie to his boss, so he devised a plan. He wrote, "My wife and I were going to have fish for dinner. So I laid down in bed and asked her to bring me the package of frozen fish we were going to eat. Then, as I remained in a prone position, I threw the fish into the air [and] caught them . . . and told her to call my boss. 'Tell him that I'm flat on my back in bed and had just thrown up my dinner,' I said. It worked. I did not have to go to work that night."[11]

Neglecting the Truth

Third, we lie by knowingly *neglecting the truth*. When we allow falsehoods to go unchallenged, we become accomplices in spreading lies. In Ephesians 4:25, the apostle Paul said we should "[lay] aside falsehood." But he also said, "Speak truth." We should never be silent when we know the truth is being contradicted or twisted.[12] In fact, Moses told the Israelites that in a court of law, "If you are called to testify about something you have seen or that you know about, it is sinful to refuse to testify, and you will be punished for your sin" (Lev. 5:1 NLT). If you know someone is being slandered and you remain silent, you are complicit in that slander.

Years ago, I was talking with a friend about a staff member at another church who had left. My friend said, "I was talking to so-and-so, and he said this staff member had to leave because of moral reasons." I explained to my friend that I happened to know a little bit about the situation, and there wasn't any moral impropriety involved. Now, my friend could've just let it go, but he decided it wasn't right for that person's reputation to be damaged. So my friend called the person who had given him the misinformation and said, "My pastor has some information to the contrary. That isn't what really happened in that situation." That's a great illustration of not neglecting the truth. The easiest thing for my friend would've been to let it go, but when somebody's reputation is at stake, we have a responsibility to stand up for the truth. To neglect the truth, staying silent when lies are being told, is to be guilty of spreading falsehood.

Inflating the Truth

Fourth, we lie by knowingly *inflating the truth*. We exaggerate. I'm tempted to do this for two reasons: I'm a Texan and we're known for telling tall tales, and I'm a preacher and we're known for making a story sound better than it really is.

Speaking of stories, I remember one about a pastors' convention. A group of pastors were in the hallway talking, and one said to another, "How many are you running in Sunday school these days?" "Oh, somewhere between four and five hundred," his friend replied. "Really? That's great." After the convention, the pastor who asked about his friend's Sunday school attendance opened his mail and saw his friend's church bulletin, which listed the attendance at 137. The pastor called his friend and said, "Hey, the other day you said you were running between four and five hundred in Sunday school. But your bulletin says 137. What's going on?" His friend said, "Well, 137 is between four . . . and five hundred."

We see this kind of exaggeration all the time. People inflate their résumés, exaggerating their work experience or their educational experience. People inflate their relationships. They say, "Oh, so-and-so is a wonderful friend of mine," when, in fact, they barely even know the person. Sometimes we exaggerate to defend our position. A husband and wife who are engaged in an argument might say, "You *always* do this and that!" Well, rarely does somebody *always* do something. Or they say, "You *never* do this or that!" Again, rarely do we never do something.

You may be saying, "Wait a minute, Pastor. Aren't you being picky here? What's wrong with a little exaggeration now and then?" The problem is that whenever we knowingly contradict, twist, neglect, or inflate the truth, we're engaged in some form of deception, which hurts our credibility as truth-tellers. Worse still, it hurts our credibility as followers of *the* Truth—Jesus Christ (John 14:6). Lying damages our dependability as witnesses for Christ.

I remember years ago telling a personal story during a sermon that sounded farfetched but was true. Later, at a church luncheon, I overheard a boy ask his father, "Dad, do you think that really happened to Pastor Jeffress?" His dad said, "Of course not, son. That was just preacher talk." It stopped me in midbite and made me wonder, *What else do I say that people think is just "preacher talk"?*

If we can't be trusted to tell the truth in every area, how can we be trusted in the important areas? That's why James gave this simple word to us: "But above all, my brethren, do not swear, either by heaven or by earth or with any other oath; but your yes is to be yes, and your no, no, so that you may not fall under judgment" (5:12). This verse isn't an absolute prohibition against taking an oath in court; even Jesus took certain oaths. This verse means we ought to be people of such integrity that the old-fashioned notion of our word being our bond is absolutely true. We shouldn't have to convince people we're telling the truth. Rather, we must be scrupulous truth-tellers, as James said, by letting our yes be yes and our no be no.[13]

Comments about Bearing False Witness, Specifically

The ninth commandment, "You shall not bear false witness against your neighbor," is found in Exodus 20:16 and repeated in Deuteronomy 5:20. However, the emphasis in these two passages is slightly different because the Hebrew words translated "false" are different in each verse. In Exodus the word is *sheqer*, meaning "falsehood," "deception," or "fraud." In Deuteronomy the word is *shav*, meaning "empty," "vain," or "worthless." Taken together, "bearing false witness" refers to any untruth, whether through evasion ("spinning" the truth), slander (passing on worthless tidbits about someone), or outright lying, with the intent to deceive or defraud someone. Bearing false witness against others has societal and individual consequences, both of which are detrimental and destructive.

Bearing False Witness Perverts Justice

Remember, the Ten Commandments were originally given to the Israelites to govern the citizens' and the community's behavior when they entered the promised land. These commands were intended to set Israel apart from their surrounding pagan neighbors—to demonstrate what it meant to live as the people of God and to bear witness to His grace, mercy, and justice in the hope that others might come to faith in Him.

However, the Lord was under no illusions that His people would live up to these commands perfectly. God knows and understands the human heart and its attraction to sin—even to sins that might incur the death penalty, like murder and adultery.

God was (and is) never flippant when it came to imprisoning or taking a human life, even if justified. That's why He commanded such adherence to the truth, because bearing false witness against someone—lying about them—could lead to their wrongful incarceration or execution. In fact, the command could be translated with a judicial slant: "You shall not provide false or misleading evidence against an accused." Truth-telling is vital to ensuring justice for the defendant and the plaintiff, just as witnesses were warned in Exodus 23 about deliberately distorting the truth (v. 1), succumbing to outside pressure to see either an innocent person found guilty or a guilty person found innocent (v. 1), and following popular opinion rather than following the truth (v. 2). That's why, in American courts, witnesses used to be charged with placing their hand on the Bible and swearing to "tell the truth, the whole truth, and nothing but the truth, so help me God." Today we've gotten rid of the Bible and God in our courts, but witnesses are still sworn to "tell the truth, the whole truth, and nothing but the truth, under the pains and penalties of perjury."

In ancient Israel, to ensure the accused wasn't railroaded into a guilty verdict or let go scot-free, the Lord required more than one witness to testify. He said, "On the evidence of two witnesses or three witnesses, he who is to die shall be put to death; he shall not be put to death on the evidence of one witness" (Deut. 17:6). Thus, to wrongly accuse an innocent person was to be, in fact, guilty of their murder. However, since even two or three witnesses could conspire against an innocent person,[14] the Lord made the accusers also the executioners: "The hand of the witnesses shall be first against him to put him to death, and afterward the hand of all the people" (v. 7). The ones to cast the first stones were the witnesses, which was intended to send a shiver down their spines and cause them to make 100 percent certain their accusation was spot-on. If the accusers were lying, then they would be accomplices to murder, for which they, too, could be executed. Bible teacher Warren Wiersbe got this right when he wrote, "Speaking the truth and honoring promises is the cement that holds society together. To tell lies in court is to undermine the very law itself. . . . It's one thing to lie, but quite something else to kill in order to protect your lie."[15]

Bearing False Witness Robs Reputations

When you defame someone—bearing false witness against your neighbor—you're guilty of robbing them of their reputation. Here's what Peter said about it: "[Put] aside all malice and all deceit and hypocrisy and envy and all *slander*" (1 Pet. 2:1).[16] The word *slander* refers to speaking out against others. But to understand the biblical concept of slander, you need to understand something about its kissing cousin: gossip. *Gossip* comes from the Greek word *psithuris*, pronounced *p-sith-ur-is*. It's an onomatopoeia, a word that sounds like what it's describing. *Psithuris*—gossip—makes that *psst, psst, psst* sound, as in "Psst! Do you want to know a secret? Let me tell you about . . ."

Secret communication about another person, whether true or false, is gossip. And it's sinful. "The words of a whisperer are like dainty morsels," Solomon wrote, "and they go down into the innermost parts of the body" (Prov. 18:8).

But when we engage in slander, we don't do it secretly. We're happy to speak out openly and spread lies about others as a farmer spreads seeds. The apostle James said not to do that: "Do not speak against one another, brethren. He who speaks against a brother or judges his brother, speaks against the law and judges the law; but if you judge the law, you are not a doer of the law but a judge of it. There is only one Lawgiver and Judge, the One who is able to save and to destroy; but who are you who judge your neighbor?" (4:11–12).

The problem with slander is it requires us to make a judgment about another person we're not capable of making, often because we don't have the whole story. Yet we continue to speak openly about others in a derogatory manner, robbing them of their reputations. There's only one person who knows the full story of another's life: God. So don't presume to know more than God about what's happening with another person and then judge them harshly by telling others what you "know to be true."

I was in a meeting this week that got a little tense while discussing an issue that needed to be resolved. As these things sometimes happen, the discussion turned into an argument that went off the rails. We were no longer talking about the issue at hand but were judging and assuming the wrong motives of the people we disagreed with. When it was my turn to speak, I had a word for the group, directed toward myself as much as anyone. I said, "There are strong feelings in this room. Some are for one thing and some are for another thing. Regardless, let's don't vilify each other. Others may be wrong—dead wrong—but so might you. Nevertheless, let's don't ascribe the worst motives to each other. Let's don't say they're for or against this measure because they're bad or stupid or uninformed or wicked. Instead, let's ascribe to each other the highest motives. Let's believe the best about each other, even if we disagree."

There's nothing wrong with disagreement. But there's nothing right about discord and destroying someone's reputation while disagreeing. Words spoken can never be taken back—just ask Raymond Donovan. He was secretary of labor under President Reagan. Indicted by a grand jury for fraud, he resigned in shame, his name in tatters. He was later acquitted but was haunted by the slander that robbed him of his reputation. At the press conference after his acquittal, Donovan made a comment that I've never forgotten. He said, "Can somebody please tell me what office I go to to get my reputation back?"[17]

There is no such office.

A good name is all any of us really possesses. Solomon put it this way: "A good name is to be more desired than great wealth" (Prov. 22:1). Here's how it was carved on a tombstone: "Praises on tombs are trifles vainly spent: A man's good name is his best monument."[18]

Each of us lives and dies with our name—it's the only one we have. So let's put a bit in our mouths (James 3:3) and control our tongues. Let's not rob each other of our reputations by bearing false witness.

10

The Tenth Commandment: Control Yourself and Be Content

You shall not covet your neighbor's house; you shall not covet your neighbor's wife or his male servant or his female servant or his ox or his donkey or anything that belongs to your neighbor.

Exodus 20:17

Pahóm was a poor Russian peasant whose greatest desire was to be a landowner. One day, after toiling in the hot sun on someone else's land, he was bemoaning his station in life. Unbeknownst to Pahóm, the devil decided to pay him a visit that day. The devil overheard Pahóm say, "If I had plenty of land, I shouldn't fear the devil himself!" Well, a sinister smile crossed the old devil's face because he took Pahóm's statement as a diabolical challenge.

All right, the devil said to himself. *We will have a tussle. I'll give you land enough; and by means of that land I will get you into my power.*

It just so happened in the coming days a piece of property came up for sale. Pahóm sold a colt and a portion of his produce, hired out his son as a laborer and took his wages in advance, and borrowed the rest of the money to buy forty fine acres. Within a year, Pahóm paid off his debts. His great desire had been fulfilled, and he was content—for a while. In time, he desired to acquire more land. He heard about a place where he could buy as much land as he wanted, "almost for nothing," from a people, he was told, who were "as simple as sheep." When Pahóm arrived at that place, he was told he could have as much land as he desired. "You have only to point it out with your hand and it is yours," he was told. The price was "one thousand rubles a day." This confused Pahóm. "A day?" he asked. "What measure is that? How many acres would that be?"

"We do not know how to reckon it out," they said. "We sell it by the day. As much as you can go round on your feet in a day is yours, and the price is one thousand rubles a day."

Pahóm thought he could cover a lot of ground in a day, so he agreed to the bargain. There was only one caveat, they told him: "If you don't return on the same day to the spot whence you started, your money is lost."

Agreed. They would start early the next day, and Pahóm would mark out his land. Before the sun rose, Pahóm paid the price and began to walk over a vast tract of a fertile property.

But as he walked he discovered new tracts that were more beautiful and bountiful than the original tract, so he decided to incorporate those into his holdings. On he walked, finding even more handsome and abundant tracts of land he wanted to own. As he walked, the day began to wane and he saw that he was a long way off from where he began, so he decided to head back to the beginning spot. But he kept seeing other pieces of property he wanted and tried to encompass them into his holdings. Then he noticed the sun was setting fast and ran toward the place where he began. He threw off his coat and boots, anything that might hinder him from getting back before sunset.

Leo Tolstoy, who wrote this tale of the land-hungry peasant, said, "Pahóm went on running, his soaking shirt and trousers stuck to him, and his mouth was parched. His breast was working like a blacksmith's bellows, his heart was beating like a hammer, and his legs were giving way as if they did not belong to him. Pahóm was seized with terror lest he should die of the strain." Just before the sun dipped below the horizon, Pahóm lunged and reached the spot where he had begun. But when the people tried to raise him up and congratulate him, they discovered Pahóm was dead.

Tolstoy's story is titled "How Much Land Does a Man Need?" He answered that question in the last line of his tale: "Six feet from his head to his heels was all he needed."[1]

The Greek sage Epicurus once quipped, "To whom little is not enough nothing is enough."[2] Pahóm was consumed with covetousness and lost control of himself, and it cost him his life. He should've been content with what he had—the original forty acres—and been happy. That's the secret to contentment: learning to want what you have. Contentment is the key to happiness in life, but there are very few people who ever experience it.

This is the subject of the tenth commandment: "You shall not covet your neighbor's house; you shall not covet your neighbor's wife or his male servant or his female servant or his ox or his donkey or anything that belongs to your neighbor" (Exod. 20:17). The tenth commandment reminds us that the greatest enemy to our happiness in life is being discontent with our circumstances.

One of the interesting aspects of this commandment is that it was given to a people who didn't yet possess the entire inventory listed in the commandment. They didn't possess houses or servants, but they would when they entered the promised land. The Lord was preparing them with a preemptive warning to be on their guard because "the human heart is the most deceitful of all things, and desperately wicked. Who really knows how bad it is?" (Jer. 17:9 NLT). Well, the Lord does—that's why He gave the commandment even before the Israelites knew they needed it.

Something else that's interesting is that in many ways the first and tenth commandments are similar and serve as book-ends to the entire list. The first commandment reminds us of the greatest commandment—to love God with our whole being (Deut. 6:5). The tenth commandment reminds us of the second greatest commandment—to love our neighbor as ourselves (Lev. 19:18).[3] Both the first and the tenth commandments address *attitudes* of the heart, while the other eight commandments address *actions* that spring from the heart. As Bible teacher Warren Wiersbe said, "Covetous people will break all of God's commandments in order to satisfy their desires, because at the heart of sin is the sin in the heart."[4]

What Does It Mean to "Covet"?

Covetousness is *not* the same as desire. In their proper place and used for their proper purpose, desires are good and godly—shelter when you need protection, food when you need sustenance, clothing when you need warmth, intimacy when you need companionship, and mercy when you need forgiveness.

Covetousness is desire gone awry. It's an excessive or obsessive desire for what doesn't belong to you. It's a form of envy and greed that wants what it can't have because it belongs to another person. As Dennis Prager noted, "To covet is much more than 'to want.' The Hebrew verb, *lachmod*, means to want to the point of seeking to take away and own something that belongs to another person."⁵ It's a narcissistic longing to fulfill self-centered desires with another person's possessions—selfish and evil desires that can lead to selfish and evil deeds.

It's important to remember that every sin you and I commit originates in the mind. All sin is rooted in the idea that God can't be trusted. We think the reason God placed these laws in His Word, the reason He says no to certain attitudes and behaviors, is that He's trying to shortchange and cheat us from something. And it's usually our desire for more that leads to all other sins.

I think there's a reason that this sin is the climax of the Ten Commandments. When you think about it, it's that desire for what someone else has that's the foundation for adultery, and many times for murder, lying, and theft. As the commandment itself states, we can covet another person's spouse, another person's possessions, another person's means of provision, or anything another person owns. Though coveting begins in the mind, it often works itself out through the hands—and violates the other commandments.

In the Bible, David is a perfect example of this. He took Bathsheba, who wasn't his wife (breaking the eighth commandment against theft), slept with her (breaking the seventh commandment against adultery), and then, to cover up her pregnancy so he could take her as his own, arranged to have her husband, Uriah, killed (breaking the sixth commandment against murder)—all because he coveted his neighbor's wife (breaking the tenth commandment). You can look throughout the Bible and find other examples of how violating the tenth commandment led to violations of the other commandments:

- Adam and Eve coveted the divinity and immortality of God, so they ate the forbidden fruit and then blamed others for their sin, violating the first and ninth commandments (Gen. 3:1–6, 12–13).
- Achan coveted the wealth of Jericho, so he stole it, violating the eighth commandment (Josh. 7:10–26).
- Ahab coveted Naboth's vineyard, so he falsely accused him, had him executed, and took his vineyard, violating the ninth, sixth, and eighth commandments (1 Kings 21:1–16).
- Ananias and Sapphira coveted the glory and honor Barnabas received, so they lied about their gift to the church, violating the ninth commandment (Acts 5:1–10).

As you can see, coveting is a serious sin and is forbidden throughout Scripture.[6] In fact, covetousness is so serious the

Lord pronounces woe—divine damnation—on those who do not control their lust for other people's possessions. Here's what He said in Micah 2:1–2: "Woe to those who scheme iniquity, who work out evil on their beds! When morning comes, they do it, for it is in the power of their hands. They covet fields and then seize them, and houses, and take them away. They rob a man and his house, a man and his inheritance."

It's been said, "All sin is contempt for God." The first sin certainly was rooted in this idea. The cause of Satan's demotion from heaven was a mixture of pride and covetousness. Lucifer (Satan's name before he was tossed out of heaven), in all his majesty and beauty as an angel, coveted the Lord's majesty and beauty. Lucifer grew discontented and conceived in his heart evil thoughts: "I will ascend to heaven; I will raise my throne above the stars of God, and I will sit on the mount of assembly in the recesses of the north. I will ascend above the heights of the clouds; I will make myself like the Most High" (Isa. 14:13–14). His reward for his pride and covetousness— his contempt for God—was to be cast out of heaven. "How you have fallen from heaven, O star of the morning, son of the dawn! You have been cut down to the earth, you who have weakened the nations!" (v. 12).

Contempt for God is serious sin. But such contempt has a way of compounding itself, whereby contempt for God leads to contempt for others. The outworking of contempt, as we've already seen, is in covetousness.

What Does Covetousness Feed On?

Fire needs fuel to burn. Without fuel, a warm, inviting fire in the fireplace or a campfire will eventually extinguish itself. However, with too much fuel, a fire can become uncontrollable.

If left unchecked, it can consume a home, a prairie, or an entire forest.

The sin of covetousness is very much like a fire. The spark that ignites it, as James pointed out, is our own sinful desires—our uncontrollable lusts (1:14–15). But like a fire, covetousness needs fuel to keep ablaze. Let's look at three sources of fuel covetousness feeds on.

Culture

We live in a culture that breeds covetousness. We see it all around us. Young people struggle with body image—the desire to look like what passes for beauty and sensuality as seen on magazine covers and in social media. Do you know what the basis of all advertising is? To try to raise your level of discontent. Advertisements seek to make you dissatisfied with your present situation so you will desire and buy their product. If only you could have that car. If only you could have that home. If only you could have that new device. Then you would really be happy. You just need something different from what you have to truly be satisfied. I like what Christian philosopher Peter Kreeft said about advertising: "The world's oldest profession is advertising. It was invented by the devil in Eden: 'See this apple? Eat it and you'll be like God.'"[7]

We live in a consumer culture that constantly tells us we deserve more and better. It causes us to think competitively with our neighbor. It sells us the lie that if only we could have the latest and greatest shiny object, we could find contentment. That certainly seems to be the message from the online retailer Amazon. I don't know if you've ever paid attention to their company logo, but it depicts a smile under the company's name, where one corner of the "mouth" begins at the letter A and the other corner ends at the letter Z. The message is subtle but unmistakable: "We have everything—from A to Z—to fulfill your desires and make your life happy, all at the click of a button." In fact, to make shopping on their website more convenient, and to encourage impulse purchases, Amazon has an option that used to be called "One Click" and is presently called "Buy Now," where you bypass the multistep process of placing an item in your cart and going through the checkout procedure—which would give you time to evaluate whether you really need or want the item.

It's no wonder our culture breeds discontentment. If we're not careful, its lies will creep into our souls. As a friend said, "The sins of the culture will become the sins of the Christian, and the sins of the Christian will become the sins of the church." He's right. It's biblical. The prophet Hosea said, "They feed on the sin of My people and direct their desire toward their iniquity. And it will be, like people, like priest" (4:8–9).

Dissatisfaction

We live in a culture that breeds covetousness, which in turn breeds dissatisfaction with God and His provision for us. I'm convinced most people suffer from a low-grade infection of dissatisfaction. We think God has somehow shortchanged us because our home isn't as lovely as our neighbor's home, our car isn't as fancy as our neighbor's car, or our income isn't as great as our neighbor's income. We never consider it might be one of God's great mercies that we don't have the upkeep of our neighbor's home, the repair bills of our neighbor's car, or the worry of being taken advantage of and losing an investment because of our neighbor's income.

By the way, how do you think that makes God feel when we feel like He's shortchanged us? Imagine this scenario: One day you're at home, and your children are at school. There's a knock on the door. You open the door and are surprised to see a worker from Child Protective Services standing in front of you. The worker says, "We talked with your child and decided we needed to investigate your house." You say, "What are you talking about?" They explain, "Your child said they are in a terrible living situation—they don't ever have the snacks they want to eat, they don't have all the things their friends have, and their house is embarrassing. We just needed to check that out and see if it's true." How would that make you feel? You would be pretty angry, wouldn't you, if your child was not only ungrateful for everything you provided them but also made up complaints that weren't true? I think God has the same reaction when we are constantly complaining or even feeling that somehow He just hasn't provided what we need to be happy in life.

We don't read them much anymore, but there's a treasure of wisdom in the old fables of Greek storyteller Aesop. One of his most famous deals with dissatisfaction: "A man and his wife had the good fortune to possess a goose which laid a golden egg every day. Lucky though they were, they soon began to think they were not getting rich fast enough, and, imagining the bird must be made of gold inside, they decided to kill it in order to secure the whole store of precious metal at once. But when they cut it open they found it was just like any other goose. Thus, they neither got rich all at once, as they had hoped, nor enjoyed any longer the daily addition to their wealth." The moral of the story, as Aesop said, is "Much wants more and loses all."[8]

Instead of grumbling and complaining to the Lord that He somehow isn't allowing your goose to lay enough golden eggs, you should make this your daily prayer: "Two things I asked of You, do not refuse me before I die: Keep deception and lies far from me, give me neither poverty nor riches; feed me with the food that is my portion, that I not be full and deny You and say, 'Who is the LORD?' Or that I not be in want and steal, and profane the name of my God" (Prov. 30:7–9).

Idolatry

It's true our culture breeds covetousness, and covetousness breeds dissatisfaction. But what we're really breeding is idolatry, placing our cravings above our worship, submission, and obedience to God. When we do that we are no better than Satan, who concluded, in the words of John Milton, "Better to reign in hell, than serve in heaven."[9]

Psalm 115 reminds us of the folly of idolatry, of trusting in anyone or anything other than God to satisfy our deepest needs. The psalmist said, "Their idols are silver and gold, the work of man's hands. They have mouths, but they cannot speak; they have eyes, but they cannot see; they have ears, but they cannot hear; they have noses, but they cannot smell; they have hands, but they cannot feel; they have feet, but they cannot walk; they cannot make a sound with their throat. Those who make them will become like them, everyone who trusts in them" (vv. 4–8).

That's the problem with believing that anyone or anything other than God can meet your deepest needs. Everyone who trusts in something other than God is going to be disappointed. Don't fall for the myth of more. There is no one and nothing that can satisfy your deepest needs in life other than God.

We were made for worship. The only question is, who or what will we worship? To give in to the sin of covetousness isn't so much to worship the object we covet, whether it be money or property or another's mate, but to worship our deformed desires, what Paul called "evil desire[s]" in Colossians 3:5, which he linked to idolatry. As I said earlier, covetousness is selfishness. And selfishness is at the heart of idolatry—the belief that the world revolves around you instead of God.

In his short novel *Heart of Darkness*, Joseph Conrad told the story of a man named Kurtz living in the wilds of the African Congo. Believing himself to be a god, Kurtz was consumed with owning what cannot be owned. Conrad wrote, "You should have heard him say, 'My ivory.' Oh yes, I heard him. 'My Intended, my ivory, my station, my river, my—' everything belonged to him. It made me hold my breath in expectation of hearing the wilderness burst into a prodigious peal of laughter that would shake the fixed stars in their places. Everything belongs to him—but that was a trifle. The thing was to know what he belonged to, how many powers of darkness claimed him for their own. That was the reflection that made you creepy all over."[10]

Both covetousness and idolatry come from that place Peter called the "black darkness" (2 Pet. 2:17). We who have been called by the Light to live within the Light (1 John 1:5–7) should have nothing to do with such darkness.

How Do We Starve Covetousness?

As the lack of oxygen starves a fire, no matter how much fuel is available, so contentment starves covetousness. *Contentment* is a curious word. According to one scholar, "It speaks of an inward self-sufficiency as opposed to the lack or the desire of outward things."[11] The Stoic philosophers loved this word because it expressed the central theme of their philosophy—that men and women are independent of outward circumstances, whether for good or for ill, and dependent only on themselves, on their inner circumstances, to find happiness in life. In Latin, the word is *contentum* and expresses the idea of being self-contained.

When we look at how Paul used the term in Philippians 4:11–13 and 1 Timothy 6:6–10, we discover he turned the meaning on its head. Instead of contentment being self-sufficiency, Paul said that contentment for the believer is Christ-sufficiency. He made this clear in Philippians 4:13: "I can do all things through Him who strengthens me."

As convenient as it would be for contentment to be built into our DNA, it just isn't. Paul said it's something we have to learn. "Not that I speak from want," he told the Christians at Philippi, "for I have *learned* to be content in whatever circumstances I am. I know how to get along with humble means, and I also know how to live in prosperity; in any and every circumstance I have *learned* the secret of being filled and going hungry, both of having abundance and suffering need" (vv. 11–12). The ultimate secret to contentment is being Christ-sufficient, as Paul pointed out in verse 13, learning to trust Christ and lean on His sovereignty in every circumstance.

The writer of the book of Hebrews came to the same conclusion: "Make sure that your character is free from the love of money, being content with what you have; for He Himself has said, 'I will never desert you, nor will I ever forsake you,' so that we confidently say, 'The Lord is my helper, I will not be afraid. What will man do to me?'" (13:5–6).

Of course, it's easy to say, "Just be content." It's quite another matter to actually achieve contentment—to learn it and apply it to life. To help you do that, let me offer three practical pointers from a man who, though fabulously wealthy, knew what it meant to be consumed with distorted desires and dissatisfaction—and who, in later life, learned to conquer his covetousness with contentment: Solomon.[12]

The Ability to Earn a Living Is a Gift of God

First, *contentment comes through recognizing that the ability to earn a living is a gift of God.* In Deuteronomy 8:18, the Lord reminded the people that He was the one who gave them the ability to work and provide the necessities of life. It's a divine gift. As Solomon wrote, "Here is what I have seen to be good and fitting: to eat, to drink and enjoy oneself in all one's labor in which he toils under the sun during the few years of his life which God has given him; for this is his reward" (Eccles. 5:18).

Notice God's gifts are simple gifts: food and drink—the necessities of life. We could add shelter and clothing. These are the very same things Paul said we should be content with: "If we have food [and drink] and covering [and shelter], with these we shall be content" (1 Tim. 6:8).

This reminds me of the Shaker hymn "Simple Gifts": "'Tis the gift to be simple, 'tis the gift to be free, 'tis the gift to come down where we ought to be, and when we find ourselves in the place just right, 'twill be in the valley of love and delight."[13]

That's what contentment promises and delivers: freedom from a consuming desire for what doesn't belong to us, love for our neighbor by respecting what belongs to them, and delight in what we already possess.

The Ability to Enjoy Life Is a Gift of God

Second, *contentment comes through recognizing that the ability to enjoy life is a gift of God.* Delight in what you have; don't desire what you don't have—that's Solomon's advice. "As for every man to whom God has given riches and wealth," he wrote, "He has also empowered him to eat from them and to receive his reward and rejoice in his labor; this is the gift of God. For he will not often consider the years of his life, because God keeps him occupied with the gladness of his heart" (Eccles. 5:19–20).

How sad it would be to earn a living and not enjoy the fruits of your labor because you don't earn what your neighbor earns. Yet covetousness is an epidemic. In fact, Solomon called the inability to enjoy the fruits of your labor "evil" (6:1). He explained that no matter how long you live, if you can't learn to enjoy life then it would've been better to have never been born because such a life is nothing but "vanity and a severe affliction" (v. 2). As Hans Christian Andersen supposedly said, "Enjoy life. There's plenty of time to be dead."[14]

The Ability to Live in Reality Is a Gift of God

Third, *contentment comes through recognizing that the ability to live in reality is a gift of God.* Solomon affirmed this truth with a pithy proverb: "What the eyes see is better than what the soul desires" (v. 9). We have a similar proverb: "A bird in the hand is worth two in the bush." In other words, what you have is better than what you wish you had.

I'd love to drive a Ferrari and have a beautiful vacation house in Hawaii. But I can't afford either one—and it's not likely the deacons of my church are going to give me a raise sufficient to cover those expenses. So what am I to do about it?

I enjoy the vehicle the Lord allows me to own and thank Him for the gift of being able to afford it. Likewise, I enjoy the times Amy and I can vacation in Hawaii, grateful to the Lord for giving me the ability to earn enough money for such a vacation.

Regardless of the vehicle you drive (if you have one) or the vacations you take (if you're able to take them), the point is the same: we have to live in reality. You don't own your neighbor's home or car and you didn't marry your neighbor's spouse. And fantasizing about them—coveting them—won't magically change your reality. So get over it! To live in reality is a gift of God.

We should take to heart this truth from another of Aesop's fables: "A dog was crossing a plank bridge over a stream with a piece of meat in his mouth, when he happened to see his own reflection in the water. He thought it was another dog with a piece of meat twice as big; so he let go his own, and flew at the other dog to get the other piece. But, of course, all that happened was that he got neither, for one was only a reflection, and the other was carried away by the current."[15]

The moral of this story is not very difficult to figure out: better the meat in your mouth than the meat in the mirror.

Reality is better than fantasy—it's a gift of God. Delighting in what you have is better than desiring what you don't have—it's a gift of God. The fruit of your labor is better than the fruit of another's labor—it's a gift of God. Learning to appreciate and apply these traits is the secret of contentment and the antidote to covetousness.

Modern-Day Blessings

I've always appreciated this story of legendary Green Bay Packers football coach Vince Lombardi, who dreaded losing. To overcome his fear, Lombardi developed a tradition every year at the beginning of training camp where he took his players through the basics. Lombardi assumed his "players were blank slates who carried over no knowledge from the year before," his biographer wrote. "He reviewed the fundamentals of blocking and tackling, the basic plays, how to study the playbook. He began with the most elemental statement of all. 'Gentlemen,' he said, holding a pigskin in his right hand, 'this is a football.'"[1]

This book has been a sort of announcement for us to get back to the basics of our faith: "Ladies and gentlemen, these are the Ten Commandments." It's a necessary pronouncement because, while many of us could recite at least some of the commandments, few of us have really applied all of them to our lives. I hope now, having reached this concluding chapter, you've come to realize just how important these age-old commands are to modern-day believers and have begun to experience the blessings that come through obeying them.

However, before you turn the last page and close this book, let me point out a few other blessings the Ten Commandments offer us.[2] First, *the Ten Commandments tell us what kind of people we ought to be: holy*. Theologian John Calvin summed this up well when he wrote, "It will not now be difficult to ascertain the general end contemplated by the whole Law, i.e., the fulfillment of righteousness, that man may form his life on the model of the divine purity."[3]

"Divine purity"—holiness—has always been the prime purpose God set out for His children. But we might not have known this was God's standard if He hadn't given us the Ten Commandments. Such knowledge is a blessing. But knowing something and becoming something are often two very different things. Holiness is an impossibly high bar to clear this side of heaven. Nevertheless, God calls us to holiness because we are blessed to be called His children (1 John 3:1), and we must reflect His character.[4] The best way to do that is to master the basics—to esteem God alone, worship God only, revere God's name, value God's day, honor our parents, preserve life, keep marriage holy, respect the property of others, safeguard the reputation of others, and control ourselves and be content.

Second, *the Ten Commandments tell us what kind of priorities we ought to value: God first, others second, self third*. In Paul's final letter before his execution, written to his protégé Timothy, the apostle warned the young pastor not to be caught off guard or surprised by the evil surrounding him. Paul called the times in which Timothy (and we) lived the "last days" (2 Tim. 3:1). Paul then made a list of characteristics that define the depravity of these days, explaining that such depravity is rooted in perverted love. We see this clearly in how the list begins and ends: "Men will be lovers of self . . . rather than lovers of God" (vv. 2, 4). Writing about this dichotomy, a friend said, "These bookends reveal a reversal of Christ's Great Commandment: love God first, others second, and (by implication) ourselves last. Whenever we upend the Great Commandment, our neighbors suffer . . . and the suffering visited upon our neighbors has ravaged humanity for millennia."[5]

The Ten Commandments reorient our perverted love and misplaced priorities. And in the world we live in, that's a blessing in itself. The first through fourth commandments tell us to love and honor God *first*. The fifth through tenth commandments tell us to love and honor our neighbors *second*. Then we can be concerned about our own needs.

Now, with our priorities straight, instead of bringing suffering to others and ourselves, such as getting caught in an affair and ruining our marriage and reputation or getting caught with stolen goods and going to prison, we experience the blessings of God's favor and the respect of our neighbors.

Third, *the Ten Commandments tell us what kind of people we are in God's eyes: unholy but loved*. It doesn't seem like much of a blessing for someone to point out our moral faults, but it is. It's actually an act of love. It says, "You're worth the effort to save."

Don't be deceived—the opposite of love isn't hate; it's apathy and indifference. Apathy says, "It's no skin off my nose whether you sin and go to hell. That's your business, not mine." But that wasn't (and isn't) the attitude of God when He sent His one and only Son to die for sinners (John 3:16; Rom. 8:32). Nor was it (or is it) the attitude of Jesus when He gave His life as a ransom to save sinners (Mark 10:45). And once we're saved, it isn't the attitude of the Father toward His wayward children, as the writer to the Hebrews explained:

> After all, you have not yet given your lives in your struggle against sin [as Christ did].
>
> And have you forgotten the encouraging words God spoke to you as his children? He said,
>
>> "My child, don't make light of the LORD's discipline,
>>   and don't give up when he corrects you.
>> For the LORD disciplines those he loves,
>>   and he punishes each one he accepts as his child."
>
> As you endure this divine discipline, remember that God is treating you as his own children. Who ever heard of a child who is never disciplined by its father? If God doesn't discipline you as he does all of his children, it means that you are illegitimate and are not really his children at all. (12:4–8 NLT)

God has never been apathetic when it comes to our salvation and sanctification—the process by which we become holy and more like Christ. If He had, He wouldn't have sent Jesus to save sinners, and He wouldn't have given us the Ten Commandments.

So the question isn't whether or not God is apathetic toward us or indifferent to the blessings that come through obedience to His commands; the question is whether or not we are apathetic toward God and indifferent to His commands.

Jesus made it clear. "If you love Me, you will keep My commandments" (John 14:15).[6] Do you love Him? Then keep His commandments. There's no better place to start than with the ten age-old commands in Exodus 20 and Deuteronomy 5. Modern-day blessings await you at the end of your obedience.

Acknowledgments

In the Ten Commandments, God shows us how to live and love in a way that enables us to experience His blessings. I'm eternally grateful for the many blessings God has poured out in my life over the years, including the faithful men and women who consistently support, encourage, and strengthen me. Among God's greatest blessings in my life is the talented team He put together for this book, including:

Brian Vos, Mark Rice, Lindsey Spoolstra, Emma Greydanus, and the entire team at Baker Books, the best publishing partner I've ever worked with.

Derrick G. Jeter, creative director of Pathway to Victory, and Jennifer Stair, who diligently assisted in crafting and polishing the message of this book.

Sealy Yates, my literary agent and longtime friend, who consistently provides me with wise counsel and encouragement.

Carrilyn Baker, my extraordinary executive associate, who expertly oversees the work of our office with a joyful attitude, and Mary Shafer, who assists Carrilyn and me in innumerable ways.

Ben Lovvorn, executive pastor of First Baptist Dallas, and Nate Curtis, Patrick Heatherington, Ben Bugg, and the Pathway to Victory team, who extend the message of this book to millions of people around the world.

I'm deeply grateful for the encouragement and support from my wonderful daughters, Julia and Dorothy, my son-in-law, Ryan Sadler, and my triplet grandchildren, Barrett, Blake, and Blair.

And at the very top of the list of blessings I am most grateful for is my wife, Amy. Thank you for your strong support and unconditional love. You are God's greatest blessing in my life.

Notes

Age-Old Commands

1. Cathy Lynn Grossman, "Americans Get an 'F' in Religion," *USA Today*, March 14, 2007, accessed August 11, 2016, http://www.usatoday.com/news /religion/2007-03-07-teaching-religion-cover_N.htm.

2. Grossman, "Americans Get an 'F' in Religion."

3. RNS Blog Editor, "News Story: In the Supreme Court Itself, Moses and His Law on Display," Religion News Service, February 28, 2005, https://reli gionnews.com/2005/02/18/news-story-in-the-supreme-court-itself-moses -and-his-law-on-display.

4. Mount Sinai is also known as Mount Horeb (Deut. 5:2).

5. See also Deut. 4:10, 12, 33, 36; 5:4, 22–27; 9:10. God eventually wrote the Ten Commandments on tablets of stone (Exod. 24:12; 31:18; 32:16; Deut. 4:13; 5:22; 9:10; 10:1–4), which were broken when the people engaged in worship of the golden calf and had to be remade (Exod. 32–34). Forty years later, the Ten Commandments were repeated at the beginning of Moses's speech to a new generation on the plains of Moab (Deut. 5–11).

6. See also Mark 12:30–31; Luke 10:27.

Chapter 1 The First Commandment: Esteem God Alone

1. *Merriam-Webster*, s.v. "esteem," accessed November 11, 2022, https://www .merriam-webster.com/dictionary/esteem; italics in original.

2. Ronald Reagan, as quoted in Bill Adler and Bill Adler Jr., eds., *The Reagan Wit: The Humor of the American President* (New York: William Marrow and Company, 1998), 114.

3. Elizabeth Howell, "How Long Would It Take to Cross the Milky Way at Light Speed?" Live Science, July 3, 2018, https://www.livescience.com/62977 -how-big-is-milky-way.html.

4. Stephen W. Hawking, as quoted by Robert Schuller, "In God We Still Trust," *The American Legion* 143, no. 3 (September 1997): 37–38.

5. See Job 28:28; Ps. 111:10; Prov. 1:7.

6. See Jer. 3:1–10; Ezek. 6:9; 16:14–63; Hos. 2; Matt. 12:39; 16:4; Luke 11:29.

7. See Hos. 4:11–14.

8. Jen Wilkin, *Ten Words to Live By: Delighting in and Doing What God Commands* (Wheaton: Crossway, 2021), 26.

9. J. R. R. Tolkien, *The Fellowship of the Ring* (Boston: Houghton Mifflin, 1993), epigraph.

10. *Merriam-Webster*, s.v. "unique," accessed November 11, 2022, https:// www.merriam-webster.com/dictionary/unique.

11. "The Wonderful Thing about Tiggers," music and lyrics by Richard M. Sherman and Robert B. Sherman. The song originally appeared in the animated short film *Winnie the Pooh and the Blustery Day* (Burbank: The Walt Disney Company, 1968).

12. See Acts 14:15; 1 Tim. 2:5; James 2:19; 1 John 5:20–21.

13. Wilkin, *Ten Words to Live By*, 24.

14. On the uniqueness of God, see also Isa. 44:6–8; 45:5, 6, 21.

Chapter 2 The Second Commandment: Worship God Only

1. Kevin DeYoung, *The 10 Commandments: What They Mean, Why They Matter, and Why We Should Obey Them* (Wheaton: Crossway, 2018), 42.

2. Adapted from Bill Hybels, *Laws That Liberate* (Wheaton: Victor, 1985), 26.

3. *Evan Almighty*, directed by Tom Shadyac (Los Angeles: Spyglass Media Group, 2007), DVD.

4. Hating God by disobeying His commandments in Exodus 20:5 is flipped on its head in John 14:15, 21, where the disciples demonstrate their love for Jesus by obedience to His commandments. See also 1 John 5:3; 2 John 6.

5. This warning is repeated three other times in the Old Testament: Exod. 34:6–7; Num. 14:18; Jer. 32:18.

6. See also Deut. 24:16.

Chapter 3 The Third Commandment: Revere God's Name

1. "Constitutional Law: Damning Blasphemy," *Time*, May 16, 1969, http:// content.time.com/time/subscriber/article/0,33009,902576,00.html.

2. Lewis Mayer, Louis C. Fisher, and E. J. D. Cross, comps., *Revised Code of the General Laws of the State of Maryland*, vol. 1, art. 72, sec. 189 (Baltimore: John Murry & Co., 1879), 824. The Maryland Court of Appeals has subsequently declared this statute unconstitutional. See *State of Maryland v. Irving K. West*,

https://law.justia.com/cases/maryland/court-of-special-appeals/1970/258
-september-term-1969-0.html.

3. Eugene Merrill, *Deuteronomy: An Exegetical and Theological Exposition of Holy Scripture*, The New American Commentary series (Nashville: B&H, 1994), 149.

4. William Shakespeare, *Romeo and Juliet*, in *The Complete Works of William Shakespeare* (New York: Barnes & Noble, 1994), 2.1.85–86.

5. "Robert," Names.org, accessed November 10, 2022, http://www.names
.org/n/robert/about.

6. On the idea of "visiting the iniquity of fathers on the children and on the grandchildren to the third and fourth generations" see comments in chapter 2.

7. In ancient times God's name was only allowed to be spoken by the high priest, and then only on the Day of Atonement.

8. Some commentators believe the man who cursed God was unnamed by Moses because the Lord did not want the personal identity of the man to be remembered. Leaving him unnamed serves as a form of disgrace. See Richard S. Hess, "Leviticus," in *Genesis–Leviticus*, vol. 1 in *The Expositor's Bible Commentary*, edited by Tremper Longman III and David E. Garland (Grand Rapids: Zondervan, 2008), 797.

9. For passages in the Bible about swearing or cursing in general, see Ps. 141:3; Prov. 8:13; Hos. 4:2; Eph. 4:29; 5:4; Phil. 4:8; Col. 3:8; 4:6; James 3:8–10. For situations in which cursing might be appropriate, see Amos 4:1–2; Phil. 3:8.

10. J. I. Packer, *Keeping the Ten Commandments* (Wheaton: Crossway, 2007), 61.

11. See also Lev. 19:12; Jer. 5:2; Zech. 5:4.

12. *The American President*, directed by Rob Reiner (2012; Culver City: Columbia Pictures, 1995), Blu-ray Disc.

13. Wilkin, *Ten Words to Live By*, 52.

14. This section is adapted from Hybels, *Laws That Liberate*, 38–44.

Chapter 4 The Fourth Commandment: Value God's Day

1. Mrs. Charles E. Cowan, *Springs in the Valley* (Grand Rapids: Zondervan, 1997), 207.

2. See John 20:19; Acts 20:7; 1 Cor. 16:2; Rev. 1:10. For an in-depth and informative discussion of the Sabbath in the New Testament, see DeYoung, *10 Commandments*, 68–71.

3. The other is the fifth commandment. The Day of Atonement was the only other day on the Jewish calendar when work was to cease.

4. The Pharisees added thirty-nine forbidden acts to the fourth commandment, making Sabbath observation a burden instead of a blessing (Mark 2:23–3:5).

5. This is the first of seven disputes Jesus had with the religious leaders over Sabbath observance: (1) Matt. 12:1–8; Mark 2:23–28; Luke 6:1–5; (2) John 5:1–18; (3) Matt. 12:9–14; Mark 3:1–6; Luke 6:6–11; (4) John 7:22–23; (5) John 9:1–34; (6) Luke 13:10–17; (7) Luke 14:1–6.

6. See Exod. 31:12–17; Neh. 9:13–15; Ezek. 20:12, 20.

7. See Barbara Killinger, "The Workaholic Breakdown: The Loss of Health," *Psychology Today*, April 30, 2013, https://www.psychologytoday .com/us/blog/the-workaholics/201304/the-workaholic-breakdown-the -loss-health.

8. William Wilberforce, "Journal," February 8, 1801, as quoted in Robert Isaac Wilberforce and Samuel Wilberforce, *The Life of William Wilberforce*, vol. 3 (London: John Murray, 1839), 3.

9. William Wilberforce, as quoted in Robert Isaac Wilberforce and Samuel Wilberforce, *The Life of William Wilberforce*, vol. 5 (London: John Murray, 1839), 135.

10. Warren W. Wiersbe, "Exodus," in *The Wiersbe Bible Commentary: The Complete Old Testament in One Volume* (Colorado Springs: David C. Cook, 2007), 182.

Chapter 5 The Fifth Commandment: Honor Your Parents

1. Jacob and Wilhelm Grimm, "The Old Grandfather's Corner," in *Grimm's Complete Fairy Tales* (New York: Barnes & Noble, 1998), 383.

2. Packer, *Keeping the Ten Commandments*, 71. See also Rom. 1:28–32, where Paul offers a similar list, including "disobedient to parents" (v. 30).

3. This section is adapted from Hybels, *Laws That Liberate*, 58–59.

4. Martin Luther, as quoted in Leslie B. Flynn, *Dare to Care Like Jesus* (Wheaton: SP Publications, 1982), 91.

5. See Prov. 23:22.

6. Kenneth S. Wuest, "Ephesians and Colossians in the Greek New Testament," in *Wuest's Word Studies from the Greek New Testament*, vol. 1 (Grand Rapids: Eerdmans, 1979), 136, emphasis in original.

7. It could be argued that the second commandment, against worshiping idols, actually is the "first" commandment with a promise, of either punishment or blessing (Exod. 20:4–6). What Paul means is that the fifth commandment is the "first" in the sense that it applies to children and the honor due to parents.

8. "Melissa Harris-Perry Promo," YouTube video, 0:37, uploaded by Choice Media, April 9, 2013, https://www.youtube.com/watch?v=3yumzS-i8XE.

9. Packer, *Keeping the Ten Commandments*, 73–74.

10. Wiersbe, "Exodus," 182.

11. I realize that some children live in homes in which they're being abused physically and emotionally. The command to "honor" their parents doesn't require them to endure such abuse. Instead, they should be encouraged to report

abuse to another parent, relative, or family friend. For adults who endured abuse as a child, honoring your parents—whether they're alive or dead—doesn't require whitewashing abuse. But amid the horrific trauma to which a parent subjected you, there are usually some good qualities for which you might be able to honor him or her. Thanking God for those good qualities or experiences can be therapeutically healing for you, while at the same time acknowledging, rather than overlooking, the hurtful experiences.

12. This same episode is captured in Matt. 15:3–6, though without the warning. The promise of punishment isn't found in the original commandment in Exod. 20:12; however, like Lev. 20:9, there are other Old Testament passages that warn of impending punishment for dishonoring parents through physical (Exod. 21:15) and verbal abuse (v. 17; Prov. 20:20).

Chapter 6 The Sixth Commandment: Preserve Life

1. Cormac McCarthy, *The Road* (New York: Alfred A. Knopf, 2018), 234.

2. Capital punishment is also alluded to in the New Testament, in Romans 13:4, where Paul spoke of governmental authority, given by God, to "bear the sword" as "an avenger who brings wrath on the one who practices evil." The principle of *lex talionis* also applies here—life for life (Lev. 24:18–21)—which was meant to ensure that punishment was appropriately proportional.

3. Though *ratsach* can refer to manslaughter, murder is the only form of killing that is prohibited since it is a willful and premeditated act, whereas manslaughter cannot be foreknown or planned because it is accidental, so it doesn't make sense to prohibit it.

4. Julie Gossack, as quoted in DeYoung, *10 Commandments*, 99.

5. States with current euthanasia laws include California, Colorado, Hawaii, Maine, New Jersey, New Mexico, Oregon, Vermont, and Washington.

6. John Calvin, as quoted in DeYoung, *10 Commandments*, 100.

7. Robert Jeffress, *18 Minutes with Jesus: Straight Talk from the Savior about the Things That Matter Most* (Grand Rapids: Baker Books, 2022).

8. John Calvin, *Institutes of the Christian Religion*, translated by Henry Beveridge (Peabody, MA: Hendrickson, 2008), 2.8.39. See also Exod. 21:14; Num. 35:20–21; Deut. 27:24 for examples of Old Testament motivations for murder.

9. See also James 2:15–16; 1 John 3:17.

10. "Watch Aid Worker Risk His Life to Save Little Girl in Mosul," YouTube video, 3:50, uploaded by Fox News, June 29, 2017, https://www.youtube.com /watch?v=3oDZQ2PvdYs.

11. See also Lev. 24:17, 21; Num. 35:16–21, 30–31; Deut. 27:24.

12. The exception to this seems to be in the case of troublesome livestock that are known to be aggressive and that haven't been properly confined. If the animal escaped and killed someone, the animal was to be stoned to death, along with the owner, unless the bereaved family demanded financial compensation (Exod. 21:28–32).

13. Larry McMurtry, *Lonesome Dove* (New York: Simon and Schuster, 1985), 418.

14. Calvin, *Institutes of the Christian Religion*, 2.8.40.

Chapter 7 The Seventh Commandment: Keep Marriage Holy

1. Adapted from Hybels, *Laws That Liberate*, 80.

2. Biblically, *adultery* also involves sexual intercourse of an engaged person with a person he or she isn't engaged to (Deut. 22:23–29). *Fornication* refers to other forms of sexual sin that don't involve a married (or engaged) person.

3. I wrote extensively on what Jesus had to say about adultery in my book *18 Minutes with Jesus*.

4. Derrick G. Jeter, *The Sanctity of Life: The Inescapable Issue* (Plano, TX: IFL, 2015), 40.

5. Jeter, *Sanctity of Life*, 40.

6. Jeter, *Sanctity of Life*, 41.

7. William Shakespeare, *Hamlet*, in *The Complete Works of William Shakespeare* (New York: Barnes & Noble, 1994), 1.5.57–59.

8. Jeffress, *18 Minutes with Jesus*, 82.

9. See 2 Sam. 12:14–16, 26–31; 13:1–14, 24–29; 15:7–18, 30–31; 16:5–22; 18:1–15.

10. Paul didn't primarily have in mind sexual lusts in the context of 2 Timothy 2; however, abstaining from such is clearly the will of God (1 Thess. 4:3).

Chapter 8 The Eighth Commandment: Respect the Property of Others

1. Stephen Sorace, "80-Year-Old Nun Sentenced to 1 Year in Prison," Fox News, February 9, 2022, https://www.fox5ny.com/news/80-year-old-nun-sentenced-to-1-year-in-prison.

2. Emma Colton, "San Francisco Defunded the Police before Reversing Course the Next Year amid Calls for 'Accountability,'" Fox News, August 16, 2022, https://www.foxnews.com/us/san-francisco-defunded-police-reversing-course-next-year-calls-accountability.

3. Murder and adultery are also rooted in contempt for others—their lives and marriages.

4. Ram Trucks, "Farmer" (television advertisement), The Richards Group, 2013. Quoting Paul Harvey, "So God Made a Farmer," as quoted in Garance Franke-Ruta, "Paul Harvey's 1978 'So God Made a Farmer' Speech, *The Atlantic*, February 4, 2013, https://www.theatlantic.com/politics/archive/2013/02/paul-harveys-1978-so-god-made-a-farmer-speech/272816/.

5. Dorman H. Winfrey, "Joiner, Columbus Marion [Dad] (1860–1947)," Texas State Historical Association, January 29, 2022, http://www.tshaonline.org/handbook/entries/joiner-columbus-marion-dad; Stanley Brown, "Let's Make a Deal," *Texas Monthly*, August 1976, http://www.texasmonthly.com/news-politics/lets-make-a-deal.

6. Packer, *Keeping the Ten Commandments*, 90.

7. Some of these are touched upon in the text, but besides direct thievery, the Bible also prohibits indirect theft, such as taking possession of lost property (Exod. 23:4–5; Deut. 22:1–4), moving boundary markers (Deut. 19:14), charging interest on loans to the poor (Exod. 22:25; Lev. 25:35–38), late payment of wages (Lev. 19:13; Deut. 24:14–15), and using false weights and measures (Lev. 19:35–36; Deut. 25:13–16). This section is adapted from Hybels, *Laws That Liberate*, 74–76.

8. Calvin, *Institutes of the Christian Religion*, 2.8.45.

9. See also Lev. 19:35–36; Deut. 25:13–16; Prov. 16:11; 20:10, 23; Mic. 6:11.

10. William Shakespeare, *Othello*, in *The Complete Works of William Shakespeare* (New York: Barnes & Noble, 1994), 3.3.155–61.

11. David Crockett, *The Autobiography of David Crockett* (New York: Charles Scribner & Sons, 1923), 132–33, emphasis in original.

12. Proverbs 6:31 indicates that thieves were to pay back seven times the amount stolen, but the ratio of seven-to-one isn't prescribed in the law.

Chapter 9 The Ninth Commandment: Protect the Reputation of Others

1. Winston Churchill, in *Churchill Himself: The Definitive Collection of Quotations*, edited by Richard Langworth (New York: Public Affairs, 2008), 45.

2. To murder someone is an extreme example of violating the sixth commandment, but Jesus tells us being angry also violates the commandment. To commit adultery is an extreme example of violating the seventh commandment, but Jesus tells us harboring lust in our hearts also violates the commandment.

3. Adapted from Charles R. Swindoll, *The Tale of the Tardy Oxcart and 1,500 Other Stories* (Nashville: Word, 1998), 344.

4. See Prov. 3:29.

5. See Prov. 12:17; 14:5, 25; 19:5, 9; 21:28; 25:18.

6. This list refers to an attitude (Prov. 6:17), a thought (v. 18), speech (vv. 17, 19), actions (vv. 17, 18), and influence (v. 19).

7. See Josh. 2:1–7; Heb. 11:31; James 2:25.

8. On God being the essence of truth, see Ps. 31:5 and Isa. 65:16. On God not lying, see Num. 23:19 and 1 Sam. 15:29.

9. Packer, *Keeping the Ten Commandments*, 97.

10. This section is adapted from Hybels, *Laws That Liberate*, 110–11.

11. Calvin Miller, as quoted in Robert Jeffress, *Heaven Can't Wait: Living the Really Good Life Now*, republished ed. (Dallas: Pathway to Victory, 2015), 67.

12. In the Bible, silence is often linked to wisdom (Job 13:5; Prov. 10:19; 17:27–28; James 1:19). However, the command to be slow to speak cannot be used as an excuse not to speak when truth is under assault.

13. See also Matt. 5:37.

14. Notable examples of innocents being falsely accused by false witness include Naboth (1 Kings 21:1–14), Jesus (Matt. 26:59–60), and Stephen (Acts 6:11–14).

15. Wiersbe, "Exodus," 183.

16. See also Lev. 19:11, 16; Prov. 10:18; 12:17; 19:9; 24:28; Col. 3:8; Titus 3:1–2; James 4:11.

17. Raymond Donovan, as quoted in Peggy Noonan, *What I Saw at the Revolution: A Political Life in the Reagan Era* (New York: Random House, 1990), 119.

18. Quoted in Jill Werman Harris, *Remembrances and Celebrations: A Book of Eulogies, Elegies, Letters, and Epitaphs* (New York: Pantheon, 1999), 278.

Chapter 10 The Tenth Commandment: Control Yourself and Be Content

1. Retold from Leo Tolstoy, "How Much Land Does a Man Need?" translated by Louise Maude and Aylmer Maude (McLean, VA: The Trinity Forum, 2005); quotations from pages 10, 15, 16, 17, 21, 22.

2. Epicurus, as quoted in William Barclay, *The Letters to Timothy, Titus, and Philemon, The New Daily Study Bible* (Louisville: Westminster John Knox Press, 2003), 145.

3. See also Matt. 22:34–40.

4. Wiersbe, "Exodus," 183.

5. Dennis Prager, *The Ten Commandments: Still the Best Moral Code* (Washington, DC: Regnery, 2015), 86.

6. See for example Ps. 10:3; Mark 7:21–23; Luke 12:15; Rom. 1:28–29; Eph. 5:3, 5; 1 Tim. 6:9–10; 2 Tim. 3:1–5.

7. Peter Kreeft, *Christianity for Modern Pagans: Pascal's Pensées* (San Francisco: Ignatius, 1993), 181.

8. Aesop, *Aesop's Fables*, "The Goose That Laid the Golden Eggs," edited by V. S. Vernon Jones (New York: Barnes & Noble, 2003), 15.

9. John Milton, *Paradise Lost* (Oxford: Oxford University Press, 2005), 1.263.

10. Joseph Conrad, *Heart of Darkness* (New York: Everyman's Library, 1967), 68.

11. Kenneth S. Wuest, "The Pastoral Epistles in the Greek New Testament," in *Wuest's Word Studies from the Greek New Testament*, vol. 2 (Grand Rapids: Eerdmans, 1979), 94.

12. I'm grateful to Derrick G. Jeter for many of the ideas in this section, adapted from his sermon "Bricks of Gold and Cobblestones of Contentment," delivered to Coffee House Fellowship, Stonebriar Community Church, Frisco, Texas, January 15, 2012.

13. Joseph Brackett, "Simple Gifts," https://hymnary.org/text/tis_the_gift _to_be_simple, public domain.

14. As quoted in Os Guinness, *Carpe Diem Redeemed: Seizing the Day, Discerning the Times* (Downers Grove, IL: InterVarsity, 2019), epigraph.

15. Aesop, "The Dog and His Reflection," *Aesop's Fables*, 94.

Modern-Day Blessings

1. David Maraniss, *When Pride Still Mattered: A Life of Vince Lombardi* (New York: Simon & Schuster, 1999), 274.

2. I'm grateful to J. I. Packer for these general ideas, which I've adapted and expanded upon, from *Keeping the Ten Commandments*, 109–13.

3. Calvin, *Institutes of the Christian Religion*, 2.8.51.

4. See Lev. 11:44–45; Matt. 5:48; 1 Pet. 1:14–16.

5. Derrick G. Jeter, *Paul's Swan Song: A Study of 2 Timothy* (Plano, TX: IFL, 2015), 104.

6. See also John 14:21; 1 John 5:3; 2 John 6.

About the Author

Dr. Robert Jeffress is senior pastor of the sixteen-thousand-member First Baptist Church, Dallas, Texas, and is a Fox News contributor. He is also an adjunct professor at Dallas Theological Seminary. He has made more than four thousand guest appearances on various radio and television programs and regularly appears on major mainstream media outlets, such as Fox News Channel's *Fox and Friends, Hannity, Fox News @ Night* with Shannon Bream, and *Justice with Judge Jeanine*, as well as ABC's *Good Morning America* and HBO's *Real Time with Bill Maher*.

Dr. Jeffress hosts a daily radio program, *Pathway to Victory*, that is heard nationwide on over one thousand stations in major markets such as Dallas–Fort Worth, New York City, Chicago, Los Angeles, Houston, Washington, DC, Philadelphia, San Francisco, Portland, and Seattle.

Dr. Jeffress also hosts a daily television program, *Pathway to Victory*, that can be seen Monday through Friday on the Trinity Broadcasting Network (TBN) and every Sunday on TBN, Daystar, and the TCT Network. *Pathway to Victory* also airs seven days a week on the Hillsong Channel. His television broadcast reaches 195 countries and is on 11,295 cable and satellite systems throughout the world.

Dr. Jeffress is the author of almost thirty books, including *Perfect Ending, Not All Roads Lead to Heaven, A Place Called Heaven, Choosing the Extraordinary Life, Courageous, Invincible, What Every Christian Should Know,* and *18 Minutes with Jesus.*

Dr. Jeffress led his congregation in the completion of a $135 million re-creation of its downtown campus. The project is the largest in modern church history and serves as a "spiritual oasis" covering six blocks of downtown Dallas.

Dr. Jeffress graduated with a DMin from Southwestern Baptist Theological Seminary, a ThM from Dallas Theological Seminary, and a BS from Baylor University. In May 2010, he was awarded a Doctor of Divinity degree from Dallas Baptist University. In June 2011, Dr. Jeffress received the Distinguished Alumnus of the Year award from Southwestern Baptist Theological Seminary.

Dr. Jeffress and his wife, Amy, have two daughters and three grandchildren.

DR. ROBERT JEFFRESS

Pathway
TO Victory

To find more information about Pathway
to Victory's radio and television programs,
to check out their online store, or to
learn more about Dr. Jeffress, head to

WWW.PTV.ORG.

First Baptist
DALLAS